Dial M for Mentor
Critical reflections on mentoring
for coaches, educators and trainers

Dial M for Mentor
Critical reflections on mentoring for coaches, educators and trainers

Jonathan Gravells and Susan Wallace

CRITICAL PUBLISHING

First published by Information Age Publishing, Inc., USA
This edition first published in the UK in 2012 by Critical Publishing Ltd

British Library Cataloguing in Publication Data
A CIP record for this book is available from the British Library

ISBN: 978-1-909330-00-9

Cover design by Greensplash Limited
Production project management by Out of House Publishing Solutions Ltd.
Printed and bound in Great Britain by TJ International Ltd.

MIX
Paper from
responsible sources
FSC
www.fsc.org   FSC® C013056

Critical Publishing
www.criticalpublishing.com

CONTENTS

ABOUT THE AUTHORS

Jonathan Gravells M.A. (Cantab.) MSc. FCIPD. Jonathan Gravells is a management consultant who advises organizations on mentoring and coaching, and provides corporate training in this area, both in the UK and around the world. He has published several books and articles on mentoring, leadership and personal change. He is a Fellow of the Chartered Institute of Personnel and Development and a member of the European Mentoring & Coaching Council. He is also on the National Health Service Institute's register of approved executive coaches.

Professor Susan Wallace PhD. Sue Wallace holds the Chair of Continuing Education at Nottingham Trent University, UK. She has extensive experience in adult education, and has worked in an advisory role for local government. She has researched and published extensively on education, training and management of behavior, and is a popular keynote speaker at conferences.

FOREWORD

David Clutterbuck

One of my ongoing research projects is to capture stories about mentoring. The concept of an older, more experienced person guiding a younger, less experienced person through rites of passage is found in many cultures, and in many variations, ranging from the transformational and supportive to the abusive. Two examples illustrate these extremes.

> **Positive:** From West Africa. A young boy's father is dying. He tells his son: "Under the big rock outside the hut is everything you will need to become a great warrior." Encouraged by his mother, every day the child attempts to move the rock. Although he pushes with all his strength, it does not budge. Eventually, at the age of 16, he feels a small amount of give. Then at 18, he rolls the rock away and finds underneath it a sword and shield. "How will this make me a great warrior?" he asks, disappointed. "Just look at your muscles," says his mother.

> **Negative:** India (the story of Eklavya from the epic Mahabarat). The poor young boy watches the guru train the children of the king in archery. He copies what he sees and, through practice, eventually becomes so good that he is able to win an archery competition, beating all the guru's students. Buoyed up with his success, he approaches the guru to ask if he can become one of his protégés. By custom, the guru may demand a gift from new acolytes. This guru, offended at the young boy's success, tells him the gift he requires is "Your thumbs."

The word mentor comes from a character in Homer's Odyssey, where the relationship between Mentor and Odysseus' son Telemachus is a subplot to the primary story of Odysseus's struggle to return home to his kingdom of Ithaca after the Trojan Wars. The original Mentor was anything but wise. In fact, he was pretty useless, both as a regent and as a surrogate father to the young prince. The real mentor was Athena, the goddess of Wisdom, whose interventions covered the whole spectrum from challenge to nurturing, and who used Socratic dialogue to enhance Telemachus' learning.

A mentor is defined in various English and American English (Amglish) dictionaries as "a wise counsellor." Mentoring has become a meme (a powerful, self-replicating idea) in 21st century societies. It provides a conceptual antidote to the disruption of close family ties and the demands of living in an urban environment. This powerful meme offers an alternative narrative for learning between generations and between cultures – an increasing amount of mentoring is directed at diversity objectives, for example. The "ment" in mentor has two meanings. One relates to the concept of minding, as in childminding. The mentor nurtures and protects, looking after the learner, who is typically referred to as a protégé. The other meaning relates to mind, as in think. The mentor encourages the learner, usually referred to as a mentee, to develop the quality and rigour of their thinking .

But, as the two stories above illustrate, the Mentor story is itself an echo of a recurrent theme in mythology, which can be found in many cultures, in many guises. This recurrent theme contains some or all of the following ingredients:

- An inexperienced (usually but not always young) person;
- A journey (metaphorical or itinerant) with multiple challenges – a metaphor for growing up;
- A wise, usually older, friend, who helps by doing some or all of the following:
  - Providing support and encouragement;
  - Giving guidance and advice;
  - Challenging their thinking, values and behaviors; and/or
  - Acting as a role model.

In both modern and classical literature, across a wide spectrum of cultures, both positive (formative) and negative (abusive) mentors abound. In Star Wars, the young Luke Skywalker is mentored first by Obi Wan Kenobi, then by Yoda. Some of the most powerful learning occurs when the young man rejects the guidance of his mentor and pursues his own path, finding insight from reflection on his own mistakes. Other powerful Mentor-figures include Jesus, Buddha, Merlin the wizard and more recently, Dumbledore in Harry Potter. A few real people from recent history have also taken on mythical Mentor status, as a result of their impact on the thinking of others – for example, Mahatma Gandhi. My colleague at Sheffield Hallam, David Megginson, often recounts the story of when Gandhi was asked by a mother to tell her son to stop eating sweets. Gandhi demurred, asking her to come back in a few weeks time. Grumbling at the time she had queued in the hot sun and the need to make yet another arduous journey, the mother departed, duly returning some weeks later. After queuing again, she repeats her request. "Stop eating sweets", the sage tells her son. "Why couldn't you have said that the first time I was here?" "Because I was still eating sweets then!" This simple story illustrates the behavior of the mentor as a proactive (as opposed to passive) role model.

Story is fundamental to effective mentoring, not least because it is a core process in how we learn. The impact of ideas and inspirations is moderated by the degree to which they spark imagination. How often, in business decisions, does one powerful anecdote outweigh pages of statistical data? Stories also help overcome cultural myopia, because they link core values and emotions with different ways of seeing the world around us – they liberate mentors and mentees from the restraints of their own experience and culture.

There is a lesson here for everyone who engages in mentoring across cultures – while the story of Mentor may be "owned" by Western culture, it is simply one perspective of an oft-repeated theme. Understanding the stories, which shape the other partner's perceptions of the mentoring role can enrich the relationship and the quality of dialogue within it. A recent article in *New Scientist*[1] captured my own imagination about the impact of cultural myopia. The author reviewed recent studies into the ethnic and cultural basis of psychological research. It seems that almost all research has been carried out on WEIRD people (from a Western, Educated, Industrial, Rich and Democratic background) and extrapolated to apply to all cultural groups. When this extrapolation is put to the test, however, even some optical illusions assumed to be hard-wired in the human brain, turn out not to be universal. How we perceive the world and how we think varies much more than conventional wisdom would suggest. Sharing stories – and particularly *listening* to other people's stories – is a powerful tool for understanding.

Stories are also important in mentoring, because they humanize conversations. Far more of the brain is engaged when listening to stories than to dry reports! In my conversations with thousands of mentors and mentees, I have consistently found that when mentors are prepared to tell the story of their own mistakes and failures, and what they have learned from these, mentees are typically highly receptive. This is partly because the mentor has stepped down from their pedestal to reveal that they are human and flawed, but partly also because we respond better to lessons *mutually extracted* from experience than to advice *given* from experience. Once a mentor becomes cast in the role of expert, he or she has lost the plot! (My own definition of an expert is "someone, whose great knowledge gets in the way of their learning.")

In this book, Jonathan Gravells and Susan Wallace use stories from Western popular culture to illustrate important aspects of the mentoring relationship. In doing so, they throw light upon the complexities – practical, moral and behavioral – of this very special and impactful learning partnership. They present the mentor in many guises, but always as essentially human. Our lack of perfection and our willingness to strive to be something more or better than we are now are not just the engines that drive mentoring. They are also the core of every story ever told, which thrilled and inspired. In that sense, at the very least, mentoring and story are integral and have been since our pre-historic ancestors sat around the embers of a fire and awoke the aspirations of new generations.

REFERENCES

[1]Spinney, L. (2010). Who's the oddball?, *New Scientist, 13*, 42–45.

Professor David Clutterbuck is one of Europe's most respected writers and thinkers on leadership, coaching and mentoring. He has written nearly 50 books and hundreds of articles on cutting edge management themes.

He is co-founder of The European Mentoring and Coaching Council, and founder of the thriving international consultancy, Clutterbuck Associates, which specialises in helping people in organisations develop leadership and coaching skills to help others. David is perhaps best-known in recent years for his work on mentoring, on which he consults around the world.

David has been responsible for the implementation, monitoring, and evaluation of highly successful mentoring and coaching programmes in numerous organisations around the world, including Standard Chartered Bank, Goldman Sachs, Lloyds-TSB, World Bank and Nokia.

David was listed as one of the top 25 most influential thinkers in the field of Human Resources by HR Magazine, and was described by The Sunday Independent as second in the list of top business coaches in the UK.

He is an Honorary Vice President of the European Mentoring and Coaching Council and is visiting professor at both Sheffield Hallam University and Oxford Brookes University.

PREFACE

Mentoring in Popular Culture

When we first set out to write this book, our idea was very simple. We are interested in mentoring and coaching and we enjoy films and television, so wouldn't it be fun to try and write a book that combined these two things and looked a bit different to other books on this subject?

Although this was probably the most enjoyable exercise in research and data-gathering we'd ever undertaken, as we ate our popcorn and tried to remember to take notes a number of things started to become clear:

- There are actually not many examples of technically good mentoring on the big or small screen, perhaps because good mentoring does not make for especially exciting entertainment.
- A book about all the myriad ways *not* to mentor someone, might be fun to write, but what would be the point?
- It would be difficult, therefore, to use our source material primarily to illustrate matters of mentoring technique, and anyway, there are a lot of good books which focus simply on "how to."
- On the other hand, the most striking aspect of the relationships we were looking at was the way in which the stories themselves stimulated interesting questions and previously un-thought-of juxtapositions and associations.

This is not to say that there's nothing to learn about technique from the interactions of the "mentors" we've selected here, and those we have chosen to call their "learners." Although not all of these partnerships are typical of mentoring, they *are* all learning relationships in some form, and there are certainly some entertaining insights to be had into how a one-to-one learning relationship succeeds or fails. But, more importantly, there is also a whole other dimension contained in the narratives, the metaphors and the symbols apparent within these stories; and these too can shed a lot of light on our understanding of mentoring.

After all, storytelling and metaphor feature increasingly in current research into leadership and learning; and so it makes a great deal of sense to apply this same principle to a critical examination of mentoring and coaching. Moreover, as we immersed ourselves in these tales, we were intrigued by some of the questions they seemed to raise. For example:

> How realistic are our expectations of personal change, and to what extent is the flourishing self-help market responsible for this? What, if any, are the moral responsibilities of executive mentors and coaches, when it comes to global corporate wrongdoing? What should constitute "truth" and "knowledge" in a world in which ambiguity and doubt can appear more effective weapons of survival?

VAMPIRES AND ALIENS? ARE YOU KIDDING ME?

OK, we recognize that not all of the examples we draw upon are entirely serious – and, as we have said, some are not primarily mentoring relationships at all – so we have had to take a certain amount of licence. In some respects, the fact that there is a form of learning relationship at the heart of all our stories is just a useful and apposite link. It is often the themes that the story illustrates which provide the richest source of questions and challenges for those of us engaged in mentoring, in whatever context that may be. So we make no apologies for dissecting the experiences of vampires, medieval monks, organized crime barons and cartoon insects, because whilst our tone may not be universally serious, the insights we are trying to unearth most certainly are. As practising mentors, we found ourselves addressing fundamental questions about how we:

- Promote self-development and self-belief without creating dependency.
- Persevere in getting real action on changes that may be difficult for the individual.
- Encourage risk and learning, without imposing our own values or ideas.

- Balance our responsibilities to the various stakeholders in the learning relationship.
- Remain non-judgmental whilst retaining a moral framework of our own.

And, whilst we do not pretend to have found all the answers, we are pretty sure that the stories we have chosen will strike a chord with all mentors, from those just beginning to those with many years' experience, whether they work in commerce, industry, education or the public and voluntary sectors. Many of the dilemmas we explore and questions we ask will also have direct relevance to the coaching profession, as well as trainers and educators in other fields. Of course, our hope is that the diverse nature of the stories we unpick will not just open up interesting and challenging areas of debate, but will also make the learning process more enjoyable and memorable too.

SOMETHING A BIT DIFFERENT...

So, here it is: a book which we hope takes the idea of storytelling as a powerful aid to learning and change, and uses it as a catalyst for both mentors and coaches to reflect critically on their own practice. We have set out to provoke challenging questions about the way in which learning relationships are conducted, as well as offer some pragmatic insights into how those relationships can be made more successful. We hope that you find the stories entertaining and informative, and that if one or two are unfamiliar, you'll welcome a reason for watching or reading them for the first time. If you are an unrepentant fan of them all, as we are, then we hope this book will open up a further dimension to these stories that you hadn't seen before.

CHAPTER 1

TURKEY, TOMATOES AND POPPADOMS

Storytelling and its Role in Making Meaning and Learning

FRIED GREEN TOMATOES AT THE WHISTLE STOP CAFÉ

Let's begin this book with a story about friendship and personal transformation. In *Fried Green Tomatoes at the Whistle Stop Café*, a bullied and downtrodden married woman, Evelyn Couch, played by Kathy Bates, meets an old woman, Ninny Threadgoode (Jessica Tandy), who tells her a series of stories about her life in the 1930s Deep South. This 1991 film, based on the original novel by the American author, Fannie Flagg, shows how Ninny's stories help Evelyn to discover her own self esteem, and develop the confidence to assert herself and open up to new experiences. Although Ninny's role may not conform to the conventional idea of a mentor (she does not, for example, demonstrate a wish to know much at all about Evelyn), her storytelling does serve one of the key functions of mentoring, which is to *facilitate self-awareness and growth.* Towards the end of the film Evelyn, recognizing how she has grown in self-assurance and resilience, explains this process to her husband, telling him that Ninny's stories were to her like a mirror held up to her face: she took a look at herself, didn't like what she saw there, and made up her mind to change.

The idea in writing this book was to see how familiar stories, as told through popular books, films and television programs could be helpful in exploring various themes and questions about mentoring. So it seems only right to begin our exploration with *Fried Green Tomatoes,* which is itself a narrative about how stories can help change someone's thinking and outlook on life. We'll be looking closely in this chapter at the way such tales, whether told by the mentor or the learner, can be used (and abused) within a mentoring relationship. We'll be analyzing the significance of images and metaphors as signs of growth and change; and we'll be considering the opportunities which stories provide for reflection and dialogue, and for the development of emotional intelligence, of which self-knowledge and self-awareness are crucial parts.

THE MENTOR AS STORYTELLER: A RANGE OF APPROACHES

Was the dramatic impact that Ninny's storytelling had on Evelyn in any way unusual or unexpected? Well, perhaps it was not as unusual as we might think. After all, why do we tell stories? For entertainment, yes. But for as long as there have been storytellers and people willing to listen to them, their tales – whether fiction, fact, or a mixture of both – have served other purposes, too: those of instruction or guidance, or food for reflection; or even as a signpost on the way to enlightenment of one kind or another. Such narratives occupy a spectrum, it seems; from the highly directive and didactic at one extreme, to the more neutral and thought-provoking at the other. The Victorians, in particular, were great believers in the didactic uses of storytelling. Children's storytellers of that era seem to have been keen to take any opportunity to instruct and direct the young under the cover of fiction. Here, for example, is a typical narrative verse about a mischievous boy, told or read to children in mid-nineteenth century England:

> Toby climbed out through the window aloof
> To fix up a pigeon-house high on the roof,
> Where a bird getting out and beginning to flutter
> Was followed by Toby o'er roof tiles and gutter
> Till his fatal mishap, how I tremble to tell!
> Master Toby's foot slipped; to the pavement he fell.
> His mother came out, full of grief, and there found
> Her unfortunate boy lying dead on the ground.[1]

Not a very jolly nursery rhyme, certainly; but it probably kept a lot of kids off the roof. We can be pretty certain that the intent of this tale is not to provoke reflection about whether climbing on the roof is sensible or not. It is to scare the living daylights out of any child contemplating such a course of action. It would be the equivalent of a modern day "mentor" launching into an account of a sales executive/nurse/teacher/social worker – someone just like the learner, in fact – and ending it something like this:

> MENTOR: So, you see, she went and did exactly what you say you're planning to do now.
> LEARNER: I see. And what happened?
> MENTOR: She got sacked/lost all her customers/ended up in court/ fell off the roof

Now think of the fables of Aesop, or the parables of Jesus. These wise teachers told stories, yes; but stories with a purpose, designed to develop their audience's understanding and encourage them to think. They were by no means ambiguous. They each held a definite lesson. However, they moved a little further than our nursery rhyme in encouraging the listener to work this out for themselves. Nearer our own time, this less directive approach is evident in the novels of Charles Dickens, with their descriptions of corruption and bureaucracy in high places, and of the hypocrisy and complacency of those who ignored the plight of the poor and destitute. Many of his novels, such as *Bleak House* and *Oliver Twist,* were written with a conscious intent not only to entertain but also to bring real issues to his readers' attention and to thereby fuel the demands for remedy and reform.

At the opposite end of the spectrum from the *Cautionary Tale,* of which the Toby poem is a classic example, lie those stories in which the storyteller's own standpoint, like Ninny's, is much less apparent, or even hidden altogether. In such cases, the story serves merely to provoke and question, and the listener is left entirely to draw their own conclusions and develop their own perspective. Because, although all these types of story will in their own way bring about learning, it is through very different processes and to very different ends. The cautionary tale tends to teach conformity and correctness, while stories like Ninny's have an altogether more complex purpose and outcome; for they are offered as a set of clues to help the learner towards independent growth and decision-making. Generally speaking, the strength of stories, in any learning context, is that they engage with our imagination and emotions in a way that advice, information and instructions do not. Consequently, they are more memorable. However, as with other learning interventions, we must be conscious, when telling stories, of how directive a style we adopt, and whether it is appropriate to the circumstances and the learner. A more directive approach may often be appropriate in circumstances where there is a "right' or "wrong' answer, or safety is at stake (such as falling off a roof). However, it is very poor when it comes to retention of learning or the development of independent thought. For

Table 1.1

Directive ⟶		Non-directive
Instructing	Joint problem-solving	Questioning/wondering
Cautionary Tale	Parable/Social Commentary	Neutral/ambiguous account
Outcome	*Outcome*	*Outcome*
Lesson learned	Some reflection but lesson still fixed	Independent thought and ownership of conclusion

this reason, the cautionary tale perhaps belongs more in the realm of teaching and instruction than mentoring. As with all of our interventions, the more directive we are, the less reflection is exercised by the learner, and the greater the likelihood of dependency. We can illustrate this in Table 1.1.

Now, for anyone who has seen or read *Fried Green Tomatoes*, it is immediately apparent that there are several important features of Ninny Threadgoode's approach, which place it nearer the non-directive end of our story-telling spectrum. So let's look now in more detail at how Ninny's stories succeed in creating learning in ways which avoid more directive and instructional narrative forms, and encourage independence and choice on the part of her learner. How does the impact these stories have on Evelyn serve to exemplify some of the positive outcomes of an ideal mentoring process?

PROMOTING GROWTH AND SELF-AWARENESS THROUGH STORIES

When Ninny tells her stories she tells them in the third person. Instead of revealing that the story is about herself, she refers to the main character throughout as "Idgie," and it is only at the very end of the film that Evelyn realizes that Ninny and Idgie are one and the same. What is the significance of this use of third person narrative? Well, firstly it means that Ninny can present her narrative as a story rather than simply as an old woman talking about herself. Imagine having a mentor who sets out to tell you his life story, episode by episode, each time you meet him (and we've all known a few), and you can see why the distancing of Ninny's life history into a tale about Idgie would be both more compelling to listen to and in some senses would also take on the mythic qualities of fictional genres, such as the tragedy or the quest, which tell us truths about the human condition. Moreover, hearing this as a story about someone she doesn't know allows Evelyn the freedom to choose to take from it what she needs for her own growth and development. She is not presented with the dilemma of feeling she has to please Ninny by being just like her. The story isn't presented as yet another pressure on her to conform to someone else's idea of what she should be. She can take what she needs and leave the rest. She is free to grow in her own way at her own pace.

For Evelyn, Ninny's stories about "Idgie" jump-start a process through which she begins to develop four key qualities which would be positive outcomes of any effective mentoring relationship. These can be summarized as follows:

- *Growth through taking risks and being open to new experiences.* Inspired by the accounts of Idgie jumping a freight train, throwing out its cargo of food to the poor, braving bees to collect their honey, Evelyn repeats Idgie's signature phrase when insisting that she will have Ninny come to live with her, telling her bullying husband, "Never say 'never' to me!"

- *Assertiveness and independence.* Evelyn hears how Idgie refused to be bullied or browbeaten by anyone; how she stood up for her black friends and employees in the Deep South of the 1920s and 30s, battled with her friend's abusive husband, set up a business, and refused to be anything other than herself. The effect of this on Evelyn is a gradual growth in assertiveness. Eventually she is knocking down walls to remodel her house; dressing fashionably in an assertive style quite unlike her earlier "Shirley Temple" outfits; and even repeatedly and joyfully ramming a car belonging to two young women who have "stolen" her parking space and spoken to her contemptuously. The contrast with her meek, passive, bullied, inert persona at the opening of the film is dramatic.

- *The ability to cope positively with setbacks.* Idgie in the stories refuses to be beaten by anyone or anything. Ninny the storyteller, although reluctantly in a nursing home, dyes her hair purple and sticks pictures of roses on the wall of her room to replace her own, real garden to which she hopes soon to return. She remains upbeat and smiling despite her circumstances. Evelyn gradually grows to follow her example. We see her begin to smile more. She turns her "empty nest" into an opportunity for remodelling her house. And finally she turns the loss of Ninny's home, demolished as unfit to live in, into an opportunity to invite the old woman to live with her and be cared for there.

- *Reflecting on your values and priorities.* One of the major things that Evelyn learns from Ninny's stories is about valuing the important and meaningful things in life such as friendship and social justice and loyalty. She also learns about the importance of stories, the way these recur throughout Ninny's tale; tall stories like the one about the flock of ducks which flies away with the lake which has frozen around their feet. These stories are told to bring comfort, passed down from Idgie's brother, Buddy, and running like a refrain, underlining the continuity of love and relationships in the face of tragedy and trouble.

Ninny's stories do not aim to be instructional, but rather allow the learner to discover for themselves the relevance and resonance of the story for their own situation. This non-directiveness emphasizes the learner's freedom to choose. Evelyn cannot be "instructed" how to become more independent, assertive and free-spirited; this would be a clear contradiction in terms. We can see this most clearly when we compare her response to Ninny's stories with her reaction and recoil from the directive and intrusive interventions of her self-help class instructor whose idea of encouraging self-awareness is to get women to look at their vaginas in a mirror. Evelyn rejects this approach and chooses instead to visit Ninny again and ask for more stories. What the stories do is to *give her permission to grow* and to change, at her own pace and in the direction which is right for her. In fact, one could argue they go further than this, by providing role models of assertiveness and independence, and a positive celebration of risk-taking and making one's own choices in life. She has *chosen* her mentor. Long after her original reason for visiting the nursing home (accompanying her husband to see his fractious old aunt), she chooses to return again and again to hear Ninny's stories; and, through that process of storytelling, to build a strong, trusting relationship with the older woman.

So what is it about these stories that enables them to have the kind of learning impact we have illustrated?

Firstly, they are *offered*. Ninny has no apparent agenda, other than to share her experiences. Indeed, as we have already noted, her indifference to finding out about Evelyn is striking. She does not set out to impose "lessons." When she shares her "story" she is almost wondering aloud, leaving Evelyn to take what is relevant for her from the tale.

Consequently, the learner is given *choice*. Evelyn can choose what conclusion she draws and what action she will take as a result. The result of this is that she feels genuine commitment to the changes that she makes in her life.

Thus, Ninny's non-directive approach leaves *responsibility* with Evelyn, the learner, to either do something with the learning she sees for herself in these stories or not.

Finally, because they do not tell her what to do, these stories leave Evelyn with a sense of *agency*. Because she is allowed to make her own meaning of what she hears, and decide for herself what action she will take as a result, her confidence and independence are reinforced in a virtuous circle of action and personal reflection. (Your learner may eventually even outgrow *you* – just as Evelyn takes Ninny into her care at the end of the film – and that is something to be proud of.)

As mentors, if we too can follow these basic principles of *offer, choice, responsibility* and *agency*, when we use stories or even just share our own experiences, we are much more likely to avoid the potential pitfalls of preaching, imposing our own agenda and values, and stunting the learner's capacity to grow and develop under their own steam. Such an approach might sound something like this:

> MENTOR: What I'm hearing is that, for you, all of these situations have at least one thing in common. You find yourself envisaging more and more ways in which things could go wrong, until finally you're dreading the meeting, or presentation or whatever, so much that your nerves end up getting the better of you.....
>
> LEARNER: Yes, kind of...except there are times when this doesn't happen, and so I'm struggling to see the difference....
>
> MENTOR: I'm reminded of a couple of experiences, one from a friend of mine and one of my own, that may provide another way of thinking about this. Would it be helpful if I shared these?
>
> LEARNER: Yes, possibly...
>
> (Mentor relates a couple of stories, including one about a colleague whose relentless over-preparation for a second interview with a prospective employer actually served to increase her anxiety and prevent her presenting as authentic a picture of herself as she did at first interview.)
>
> MENTOR: Is there anything about this experience which feels relevant to your situation?..............(At this point, if the answer is "no', then this in itself may provoke further insight. However, if the answer is "yes', then the mentor may ask:) What, if anything would you conclude from that?.........Is there anything you might be able to do differently as a result?.......

ENCOURAGING EMPATHY AND
INSIGHT THROUGH STORIES

According to the American philosopher Richard Rorty[2], there may be another way, too, in which stories can assist in our development as fully functioning, socially responsible adults. In several of his later works Rorty argues that all progress towards empathy (understanding and feeling for the point of view of others) and social justice is best achieved not through scientific or factual enquiry, but through the imagination. Therefore, he suggests, fictional narratives such as stories and novels provide us with the opportunity and ability to relate to other people by letting us look at the world through strangers' eyes. This experience allows us to see others as "fellow-sufferers" deserving of our sympathy and understanding. To some extent, this is part of the experience which Ninny Threadgoode provides for Evelyn. The characters in her narrative become "real" for Evelyn and she is able to feel for them, despite (she believes) never having met any of them. From the very start she is reduced to tears by Ninny's account of Buddy's death. The development of empathy – the ability to imagine ourselves in another's shoes and understand their feelings and their point of view – is an essential component of that much misunderstood quality, emotional intelligence. It can be an important aspect of the mentor's role to encourage the development of emotional intelligence in the learner. Stories, with their matchless opportunity to show situations through another's eyes, can be a valuable tool for the mentor on these grounds alone.

THE LEARNER'S OWN STORY:
EBENEZER SCROOGE IN *A CHRISTMAS CAROL*

But what happens when it is the learner who is telling the story? At the last count an astonishing thirteen film versions (if we also count cartoons) have been made of Dickens's famous 1843 novel, *A Christmas Carol*. Perhaps the most faithful adaptation is the 1951 movie starring the wonderful Alastair Sim as Ebenezer Scrooge, an embittered old skinflint who, through his own cynicism and insensitivity, has alienated himself from the warmth of human companionship. When we first encounter him, his business partner, Marley, has recently died. However, on the night before Christmas, Marley's ghost returns as a dire warning to Scrooge to change his ways unless he wishes to find himself in the hellish afterlife that Marley is suffering, weighed down like a felon with the chains and coffers which symbolise his obsession with materialism and avarice while alive. In this respect, Marley's ghost is presenting his own predicament as a cautionary tale – he is here a *Master Toby* whose fate should act as a warning to others. But it is the three spirits whom Marley then sends to visit his terrified partner who prompt Scrooge into looking at his own life as a story and learning from it. These spirits – the Ghosts of Christmas Past, Present and Future, visit Scrooge one after the other and are both the facilitators of, and audience for the excerpts from his life story which they explore with him. In this sense, the Ghosts serve the same function as a mentor does in prompting the learner to tell their story and reflect upon it in order to move forward. The first Ghost encourages Scrooge to *review his past*, "taking him back" to key incidents in his childhood and young manhood – for example, the occasion on which he first makes a choice between love or money – in order to better understand what has made him as he is. The second Ghost enables Scrooge to *reflect upon his present situation*, and to begin to form some insight into how others see him.

The third Ghost pushes him to *envisage his future* and to ask himself some crucial questions:

- Where is my current trajectory taking me?
- Is this inevitable?
- What changes do I need to make to my relationships/behaviors/values/goals in order to make a more positive future likely?

The three approaches to exploring the learner's own story: *review, reflection,* and *envisaging ,* are useful ones for the mentor to encourage. The practice of envisaging the future is sometimes referred to in this context as "*visioning*", an alternative term which may have more creative and positive connotations, suggesting a greater degree of agency in bringing about the desired scenario or outcome. Another aspect of this storytelling which it is important to note is that Scrooge is encouraged to focus on *particular episodes* or *critical incidents.* He is not being urged to review every detail of his life, past and present. He looks at turning points, at key relationships, at times when significant decisions were made (or not made), and so on. This managing and containing and focusing of the learner's story can call for some skill on the part of the mentor. It means above all that they cannot take up the position of a passive listener, any more than Scrooge's Ghosts do. The mentor must use careful questioning and prompting to help the learner home in on what is of significance to their current development needs. Just sitting and listening to someone's rambling life story or series of amusing anecdotes may be polite or may be masochistic; but it's not mentoring.

As well as demonstrating the three different angles from which the learner can be encouraged to relate and explore their own story – past, present, future – the Ghosts also, in their way, typify three different ways in which a mentor may relate to their learner. The first Ghost is a little distant – it is described as somehow "receded" – but its main characteristic is to shed light. Indeed, towards the end of his encounter with this Ghost, Scrooge begs it to dim the light as it is beginning to prove painful for him. We can interpret this as Scrooge, the learner, finding it difficult to deal with or assimilate the sudden clarity about himself which this ghostly mentor has helped him to achieve. This Ghost says very little, but it does ask some questions from time to time which focus Scrooge's story and move it on from incident to incident.

The second Ghost, Christmas Present, is far more genial and unthreatening. His strategies include reflecting Scrooge's own words back to him; insensitive words of which Scrooge, on hearing them repeated like this, now feels ashamed. This Ghost also focuses on developing Scrooge's sense of empathy, showing him the impoverished but cheerful family life of his employee, Bob Cratchit, at the centre of which is Bob's much loved, disabled and – we learn – dying son, Tiny Tim. In terms of mentoring, what is happening here is that the learner, Scrooge, is being encouraged to extend the boundaries of his own story in order to grasp the fact that other people's lives are as "real" as his own, and that his actions and attitudes inevitably have consequences for others as well as for himself. In this case his dismissal of Christmas as "humbug" has meant that the loyal and unresentful Bob Cratchit has been given no extra holiday time, or money, to spend with his dependent wife and children. When the novel begins, Scrooge is entirely solipsistic. That is, he sees everything in terms of himself and his own needs. As the mentoring process proceeds, he begins to recognize this flaw in himself, and to start accommodating the needs and feelings of others into his world view. Nowadays we would say, perhaps, that he is beginning to develop some degree of emotional intelligence.

Even though this second Ghost is by far the most genial of the three, it does not pull its punches. It is never soft on Scrooge, and is unrelenting in its purpose of jolting him out of his self-obsession and bringing him face to face with stark reality. The clearest illustration of this comes towards the end of their encounter, when Scrooge notices two emaciated children cowering beneath the folds of the Ghost's cloak, "wretched, abject, frightful, hideous, miserable." They are Ignorance and Want, says the Ghost; social evils for which Scrooge had hitherto felt no concern and certainly no responsibility. The process of telling and reflecting on his own story has enabled him now to see more clearly the plight of others. But when he asks, distressed, whether something can be done to help them, the Ghost simply repeats Scrooge's earlier words back to him: "Are there no prisons? Are there no workhouses?" This is tough mentoring indeed.

The third and final Ghost, who enables Scrooge to envisage the bleak future to which his current trajectory could carry him, is entirely silent. All it does is to point. Even its face, its identity, is hidden. It serves to remind us forcibly that, in order for the learner to be able to tell their story at all, the mentor needs to shut up and listen. Clever interventions are not everything. Sometimes the most helpful thing a mentor can do is simply to listen while the learner confronts their own reality. For the storyteller to learn from the tale, to gain in self-knowledge and assertiveness, and to recognize, through reflection, what their priorities should be, it is necessary that they be allowed to talk, to tell their story and be encouraged to reflect upon it.

So these Ghosts of Christmas Past, Present and Future have a lot to teach us about how to elicit a learner's story and help them use it a means of personal growth. However, we would be ill-advised to follow their example in every detail. Of course, the Ghost of Christmas Present, who ages dramatically overnight, may simply reflect how many of us have felt after a difficult mentoring session. On the other hand, dressing in a black hood and pointing wordlessly with a skinny hand isn't always the best way to fill your learner with confidence.

Let's summarize here some of the important mentoring issues which this tale of Scrooge and his ghostly mentors has illustrated for us:

- The learner should be encouraged to tell their story in order to *review* the past, *reflect* on the present, and *envisage* the future (Is the future towards which their current trajectory is taking them the future they aspire to?)
- They should be encouraged to focus their storytelling on particular episodes or *critical incidents.*
- The mentor must use careful *questioning* and *probing* to help the learner home in on these aspects of their tale.
- By encouraging the learner to tell their story the mentor's aim is to help *shed light* on what is currently hidden from the learner's understanding of themselves and others.
- This "enlightenment" can be further encouraged by *reflecting back to the learner* attitudes they've displayed or words they've used in their narrative which are problematic.
- The learner can be encouraged to reflect on other characters in their story in order to fully understand *the reality of others' lives* upon which their own actions and attitudes have consequences.
- Learners can be encouraged, through their stories to *recognize their own flaws* or areas for improvement and to *acknowledge the needs and feelings of others,* thereby developing the ability to apply their *emotional intelligence.*
- Part of the mentor's role is to *encourage the learner to face reality,* how ever painful or difficult this may be.

SLUMDOG MILLIONAIRE: **OUR OWN CAUTIONARY TALE**

In the multi-Oscar winning 2009 film, *Slumdog Millionaire,* based on Vikas Swarup's novel, *Q and A,* Dev Patel plays Jamal Malik, a penniless eighteen year old from the slums of Mumbai. Jamal is on his way towards winning the top cash prize on India's version of *Who Wants To Be A Millionaire* when he is arrested on the accusation that he is somehow cheating. During the course of a long and initially brutal interrogation, Jamal tells the police inspector a series of stories about his life which explain how he came to know each of the answers which he gave correctly on the quiz show.

Often the stories that learners relate to their mentors can feel a little bit like this. In other words their principal purpose is exoneration. The story may therefore serve more to justify actions and attitudes than to explore and question. Learners' stories about their bosses sometimes fit into this category! Of course, in Jamal's case this is entirely understandable. The police who listen to Jamal's stories are obviously in no sense his mentors, and when you are hanging by the wrists with electrodes on your nether parts, it is not the time to reflect critically on your life, but to refute the accusations against you as convincingly as possible. So, a word of caution is appropriate here. As mentors, we must seek to understand how the learner is using their story, and remember to challenge them for alternative perspectives if required.

> I find myself getting frustrated with Patty because we spend a lot of time talking about how the Chair of Governors sidelines her, goes behind her back and generally "plots her downfall". I am sure there is an element of truth in this, just as I am sure that Patty finds it a convenient excuse for powerlessness and inaction. What is needed is a way of challenging this narrative, and encouraging her to relinquish the need to justify herself to me and reflect more on her assumptions. Actually, that makes me wonder.......Why is it that she feels the need to justify herself to me anyway? What does that say about our relationship?....

Powerful though storytelling can be in a mentoring context, this should not blind us to its potential drawbacks. Telling stories has an unfortunate association with lying and dishonesty, for example, as well as self-justification. The very nature of stories, with their engaging combination of ideas, facts, values and emotions, means that they can draw the listener in, undermining the unwary mentor's objectivity and facility to challenge or question[3].

Although Jamal's stories are episodic and tell the story of his life in flashbacks, just as some of Scrooge's and all of Ninny's do, they do not serve a developmental purpose, either for himself or for anyone else. Bearing this in mind reminds us that:

- Storytelling on its own does not necessarily serve a developmental purpose.
- Review and reflection are essential elements if the story is to help the learner to move forward, whether it is a tale told by the learner themselves or by the mentor.
- A mentor may need to reflect on the intent behind a learner's story and challenge its assumptions and perspective.

SIGNS, SYMBOLS AND METAPHORS

When we use words or images that describe something in terms of something else – for example, the greedy guy in the staff canteen as "a pig", or the head of Human Resources as "Attilla the Hun" – we are using that age-old ingredient of vivid storytelling: the metaphor. Some metaphors are pretty stale and clichéd, such as the two we've just used here; but sometimes these figurative images or connections can throw new light on a person or situation and generate insights which everyday language with its literal descriptions cannot do. Both stories we've been discussing here provide interesting illustrations of this. Look at the two main characters' names in Fried Green Tomatoes: Evelyn *Couch*? Get it? She needs to stop being the proverbial potato and grab hold of life, take a few risks, become more positive and assertive. And Ninny *Threadgoode*? Well, she spins a good tale; she weaves a good story; and her narrative is assembled a piece at a time like a good old American patchwork quilt. These names are clues which help our understanding of each character's function in the story. Names as a clue are also a vital ingredient of fairytales (of which more later) – think of Snow White or Prince Charming; and so the naming of Evelyn Couch and Ninny Threadgoode send us another signal, too: that this is a sort of fairytale – of a quest and a transformation – and perhaps one we can learn from. In *A Christmas Carol*, another fairytale of sorts, the metaphors as clues lie not in the names but in the characteristics of the Ghosts-as-mentors. For example, the beam of light which emanates from the head of the second Ghost, an illumination which Scrooge finds increasingly painful, is a literal representation of the Ghost/mentor's role both in bringing enlightenment and in making Scrooge see reality more clearly. This is a good example of a metaphor which may be interpreted in more than one way; and, exactly because it is not immediately transparent, it serves its function in making us *think and reflect* – about blind spots, truth, reality and "seeing the light."

In a very readable book called *Metaphors We Live By*,[4] two American authors argue that the metaphors we use individually and collectively – sometimes unconsciously rather than by conscious choice – can often be taken as accurate indicators of how we construe the world, and can throw some light on deeply held attitudes, assumptions and values which we might not otherwise recognize, much less acknowledge or express. Indeed, it is because we don't, as individuals, always consciously choose the metaphors we use that psychoanalysts and psychotherapists may focus on such images when they occur in their patients' conversation, recognizing their significance in providing a possible insight into the patient's preoccupations and unconscious thought processes. Although their role is by no means that of a psychotherapist (even though it may feel like that sometimes), mentors, too, can nevertheless find it extremely useful to pay close attention to the metaphors and images which a learner uses in talking about themselves and their work. Someone who speaks about their workplace in terms of trench warfare, for example (getting close to the wire; venturing into no-man's land; keeping their head down; holding the line), clearly has "issues" of one sort or another.

TURNING TRUTH INTO FICTION

The episodes from his life story which Scrooge was encouraged to replay and reflect upon were, within the context of the novel, "facts". But sometimes it can be useful to fictionalize our story; and we saw how Ninny did this to some degree by speaking of herself as though she were someone else – Idgie. This served a number of purposes, as we've seen. However, let's have a look now at what might be gained by encouraging the learner to tell a fictional tale, or to present their own experiences in the guise of a story.

This approach has been explored recently by researchers looking at ways in which professionals can be encouraged to reflect upon their performance and their working lives in order to develop the personal and professional skills and attributes necessary for their job and their career progression. This includes, for example, the way in which stories can be analyzed by the teller in order to identify assumptions which may be embedded within the narrative, but which the teller is not consciously aware of: assumptions about the storyteller's own role in the workplace, perhaps; or their expectations, or their views about what is important or of value and what is not. Discovering such underlying assumptions in their own stories can help the learner to move towards a greater self-awareness. Richard Winter and others, writing in 1999, point out that literal, factual accounts of experience (such as a learner might describe to their mentor during a mentoring session) carry with them a risk of personal or emotional exposure which may discourage the teller from including or exploring painful or potentially embarrassing episodes, or contentious issues[5]. A fictionalized account, on the other hand, can be shared and discussed in relative safety, since the teller has distanced themselves from the story. In *Fried Green Tomatoes*, it cannot be easy for Evelyn to confront the reality of where her life of meek subservience and low self-esteem has led her. The advantage of Ninny's stories is that they allow her to address this difficult and sensitive issue in an indirect way, through the experiences and example of others[6]. This same principle can be applied to learners' stories. A strategy of encouraging the learner to tell it as though it was a story about someone else can be a useful tool for the mentor in situations where the learner needs help in reflecting on issues or incidents which may be sensitive. Part of our skill as mentors is finding ways of creating this "safe space" in which our learners can reflect honestly on their experience and make meaning of it.

A recent UK study[7] illustrates clearly how both a fictionalizing of their experience by learners and an attention to metaphor can be usefully applied in a mentoring context. As an experiment to look into ways of promoting reflective practice, fifty new teachers were asked to relate their experiences of their workplace (in this case mostly colleges of further education) not in factual terms but using the fictional format of a fairy story. The purpose of this experiment was to discover whether the use of fictional narrative would stimulate their ability to reflect on their professional experiences more freely and perceptively than simply giving a factual account would do. The experiment produced some very interesting results, particularly in the metaphors these learners used to represent their students (goblins, trolls, monsters, ogres) and those used to portray their mentors (wizard, fairy godmother, knight, queen, Prince Charming) whom they clearly saw as powerful, almost magical figures whose intervention could put everything right. Here, for example, is one young teacher describing such an intervention:

> At this moment Prince Charming came charging through on his great white steed, brandishing his sword. "You see, my dear," he said to the Princess with a grin, "that's how it's done."

The potential of metaphor and fictional narrative to cut through to the heart of experience is clearly demonstrated here. A mentor, hearing a tale like this can gain significantly greater insight into the learner's preoccupations and self-image, their level of confidence or lack of it, and their areas for development. They may also get an idea of how the learner views the mentoring relationship. For example, if the mentor is simply seen as some sort of saviour or one-person task force, the relationship and the mentoring process itself clearly needs re-addressing. (As for "Prince Charming," it looks as though he may have a problem of quite a different sort on his hands). But although these sorts of insights are useful to the mentor, *they will not lead to progress unless the learner is encouraged to reflect upon them and use them productively as a way of interpreting or reinterpreting their experience.* Such insights are the first step to development and growth. Like Ninny's stories for Evelyn in *Fried Green Tomatoes*, the fairytales these young teachers told provided a mirror in which they were able to see themselves and their professional development needs more clearly and with greater objectivity than would otherwise have been possible.

SUMMARY

In this chapter we have looked at several ways in which stories can be used as part of the mentoring process. In a book about how fiction – in films, books and TV – can help us to reflect critically on key issues in our own mentoring practice, a discussion about stories of one kind and another has been inevitable. Here is a summary of what we've said about stories and the process of reflecting upon them:

- If stories are to encourage growth and self-discovery, they need to be more than mere cautionary tales.
- As non-directive narratives, stories allow the learner the freedom and choice to take from them what they currently need for their development.
- They are one way of encouraging positive risk-taking and opening up to new experience. Thus they can provide the learner with permission to grow.

- They can provide an example and inspiration in coping with setbacks.
- They can help a learner to reflect upon values and priorities.
- They can be used to help develop empathy for others.
- They provide a means of interpreting or re-interpreting our experiences.
- They can be used to envisage the future and to trigger discussion as whether the future the learner aspires to is the one to which their current trajectory is heading.
- The images and metaphors in our stories can provide us with insights into our own unconscious assumptions and values.

Of course, there is even more to mentoring and being mentored than telling stories and listening to them, as we shall discover in the chapters which follow.

REFERENCES

[1]c1850. *The Misfortunes of Toby Ticklepitcher,* March's Penny Library No. 8.

[2]Rorty, R. (1989). *Contingency, Irony and solidarity.* Cambridge: Cambridge University Press.

[3]Reissner, S. (2008). Narrative and storytelling – New perspectives on coaching. *International Journal of Mentoring and Coaching, Vol. VI, Issue 3 12/2008.*

[4]Lakoff, G., & Johnson, M. (1980). *Metaphors we live by.* Chicago: University of Chicago Press.

[5]Winter, R., Buck, A., & Sobiechowska, P. (1999). *Professional Experience and the Investigative Imagination.* London: Routledge Press.

[6]Hardingham, A. (2004). *The coach's coach.* London: CIPD.

[7]Wallace, S. (2010). Joining the goblins. *Education action research, 18*(4), 467–479.

Films and Books

Avnet, J. (Director). (1991). *Fried Green Tomatoes at the Whistlestop Café* [Motion picture]. United States: Universal Pictures, Act III Communications, Fried Green Tomatoes Productions. (Based on the novel by Fannie Flagg (1987), published by Random House, New York)

Boyle, D. (Directory). (2008). *Slumdog Millionaire* [Motion picture]. UK: Celador Films, Film 4. (Based on the novel *Q & A* by Vikas Swarup (2005), published by Doubleday.)

Dickens, C. (1843). *A Christmas Carol* . London: Chapman & Hall.

CHAPTER 2

MONKS, MOBSTERS AND THE MATRIX

Knowledge, Learning, Action and Change

THE NAME OF THE ROSE

The Name of the Rose, originally a novel by the Italian author and academic, Umberto Eco, and turned into a film starring Sean Connery and Christian Slater, concerns the efforts of a visiting Franciscan friar called William of Baskerville (Connery) aided by his young "scribe and disciple," Adso of Melk (Slater), to solve the series of grisly murders which take place in the abbey over the days leading up to a visit by a papal legation, led by the Inquisitor, Bernard Gui.

The story revolves around the fortress-like library of an ancient, and equally fortress-like, Benedictine abbey. Here is stored an enormous collection of books and manuscripts from all over the world, some of them rare or even unique. This is not a library as you or I would know it. There are no library cards or date stamps, although, to be fair, there are quite a few weird-looking people in there largely to escape the cold. There is no chance of being fined for overdue books, because you cannot really take them out. The monks copy and translate these texts, in the scriptorium attached to the library, but that's as far as they go. As it turns out, if you do take them out, the retribution is somewhat more severe than a twenty pence fine. Add to this the fact that the library is actually constructed as a labyrinth, which only the librarian and his assistant are able to navigate, and you have a pretty compelling image of the monks' approach to knowledge management.

THE TRUTH IS OUT THERE...THE KNOWLEDGE ECONOMY

Much has been written about "the knowledge economy," the idea that for many societies in the modern world wealth is about what we know more than what we make, and that more effective "knowledge management" is what we need to succeed in an ever more complex environment. But what is the role played by mentoring in all this? How do we differentiate between knowledge and learning, and what do we do with it when we've got it? Where should our focus be as mentors?

> MENTOR: There have been times in my mentoring of Jan when it's felt rather like "the blind leading the blind." What I mean is that we have found ourselves exploring complex issues which neither of us has frankly thought much about previously. This scares me sometimes, not because I feel I need to have the solutions, but because I'm not even sure what the right questions are....
>
> MENTOR: It's funny really. Meera's difficulties in establishing more productive relationships with her senior colleagues don't seem to stem from ignorance or lack of self-awareness. When we discuss rapport-building and the impact of informal networks, etc; she absolutely gets what it's about. But somehow nothing changes....
>
> MENTOR: The breakthrough came finally after several sessions, when I realized that Derek's dilemmas about future career direction and his loyalty to the organization that had trained him would not be resolved by any amount of pros and cons discussion or decision-making models. This was a heart issue as much as a head one. He needed to frame the situation in an entirely different way...."

Paradoxically, our first step in addressing this seemingly "modern world" problem is to transport ourselves back in time to the nameless abbey which is the setting for this mediaeval murder mystery.

ACTUALLY, THE TRUTH IS IN HERE... KNOWLEDGE AS POWER

At its heart, the story of *The Name of the Rose*, recounted by Adso in the first person, is a Sherlock Holmes style "whodunnit," and there are obvious echoes of this in Baskerville's name and in his relationship with Adso, his "sidekick." However, two differences make it interesting and relevant to us. Firstly, theirs is more of a mentoring relationship than that of Holmes and Watson, albeit following an appropriately mediaeval apprenticeship model, rather than the kind of equal and mutual learning relationship recognizable to the modern developmental mentor. Secondly, the story deals with themes which are directly relevant to the practice of mentoring, especially in our modern "knowledge economy." It addresses our attitudes to learning and knowledge and the way we go about making meaning and exploring the unknown.

For those in charge of the ancient abbey, as for its visitors from the papal legation, knowledge is "fixed" and static. We know pretty much everything we're going to know and furthermore it's all been captured in holy scripture. For the cruel inquisitor, Bernard Gui, as for all those portrayed as villains in the story, knowledge is a source of status and power over others, jealously guarded and hidden away. Knowledge is not there to be shared or, heaven forbid, questioned, but rather to enhance one's reputation through exclusivity of ownership. As various monks begin to turn up dead in a variety of suspicious circumstances, we learn that a common link in the chain of murders is a "forbidden book," taken from the library, despite all its arcane security arrangements. This is the supposed second book of the Poetics of Aristotle. The reason that "the authorities" see it as so dangerous is because it uses comedy and satire to incite the "common man" to question and challenge the accepted orthodoxy. Such undermining of the Church's power cannot be countenanced.

To our hero, William of Baskerville, this arrogant approach to knowledge and learning is the embodiment of evil. For him, the very idea of a book being forbidden symbolizes all that is wrong about one group of people presuming exclusive access to knowledge and "the truth." It is a fundamental conflict which we are reminded of throughout the story: in Adso's assertion that the world is beautiful, but labyrinths ugly, for example, and in the contrast between William and Adso's genuine thirst for learning and assistant librarian Benno's "lusting after" knowledge for the power it bestows.

THE TRUTH IS FOR YOU TO DECIDE – KNOWLEDGE IN MENTORING

For the mentor, the idea of knowledge being something to be shared rather than wielded, may appear to go without saying. Surely, there are no mentors out there who believe otherwise? Well, hopefully not, but there may be the odd one who subscribes to the view that knowledge is static. In other words,

> MENTOR: I've spent a 25-year career learning about leadership/marketing/work-life balance/strategic decision-making, and now it's time to pass that knowledge on to another generation...."

What our monkish sleuths are trying to say is that not only should knowledge be shared because that allows us all to benefit, but that the very process of sharing knowledge continually develops and improves it, as competing perspectives, ideas and hypotheses are discussed and refined. Knowledge is living and constantly changing, and if the worst crime is hiding it away, the second worst is assuming we've somehow captured it all. Just as circumstances, perspectives and experiences change, so our knowledge must adapt and develop. Universal laws and a stable "truth" may be a seductive idea, but, for William, they prove elusive in reality. As we examine or experiment with something we change it. What is more, the complacency of "one truth" prevents us from learning more. It closes our minds to the multitude of possibilities which it is part of every mentor's role to bring to their learner's attention.

This is critical to the idea of mentoring. As a process, mentoring helps us to make our tacit knowledge explicit. This allows it to be shared, adapted, and developed. One could argue that it is only when we interact with information and ideas in this way that they truly become knowledge[1]. One of the perennial questions asked on training courses is "to what extent is it legitimate to share one's knowledge and experience, as a mentor?" "Where is the boundary between using one's own experience to help the learner and giving out advice or solutions?" The answers lie partly in our mindset. If we reject the idea of one universal truth, and believe that, for the learner, meaning and knowledge are best created for themselves out of the process of sharing options, ideas and possibilities, then we cannot go too far wrong.

> MENTOR: Fran and I were discussing her approach to marketing strategy. She knew that I had some experience of this from a previous life, although, as her executive mentor, I had, up to now resisted the temptation to refer to my own expertise. She was clearly struggling with how to address some of the less positive news coming out of the brand research, and actively sought some opinion from me. It's a tricky one. On the one hand, hers is a very different business from the ones I have worked in, and I know she is far more naturally creative than me; something her CEO specifically hired her for. On the other, I am being engaged to help.
>
> In the end, I persevered with challenging Fran to generate a few possible strategic responses, however ludicrous and impractical she or I thought they might be. Only then did I offer to share my own experience, if she wanted me to. I threw in a couple of things I

had tried in the past, and we added them to the list. I then stepped back and encouraged Fran to squeeze out some more thoughts before getting her to make some decisions about "reality checking" and prioritizing all these options. As it turned out, one of her early thoughts, which I'd secretly considered a complete non-starter, proved to be a key part of their eventual recovery.

Our mentor here is careful to approach the business of building knowledge in an appropriate way. She doesn't provide "the answer" or assume that what worked for her will work for someone else. She avoids the temptation to venture further into teaching mode by challenging the learner to use these additional inputs as a springboard for more of her own ideas. Finally, the ultimate decisions about priorities and actions are entirely the learner's.

THE TRUTH IS NOWHERE –
AMBIGUITY, ENQUIRY AND CONTINUOUS LEARNING

This idea of individuals making their own sense of the world and being free to determine their own truth is apparent in William's approach to the books in the abbey's library. For him they consist of signs and symbols, of which we must each make meaning, and therefore interpretations will inevitably differ. Adso puzzles over William's unwillingness to discriminate between faith and heresy during one of the many lengthy discussions about supposedly heretical Christian sects. When the Abbot asks him where the truth lies, William replies that at times it is "nowhere." We assume that William abandoned his dark past as an Inquisitor as a result of realizing that truth and reality are relative. When Bernard Gui extracts the supposed "truth" from a member of the abbey's staff by torture, William is characteristically dismissive of its worth.

Though mentoring might occasionally feel like torture (to either party), the lesson for us here is about the power of not knowing and the essential role this plays in continuous learning. For William, books are not there to be believed, but to be "subjected to enquiry." (You might bear that in mind whilst reading this). It is perhaps no surprise, then, to discover that William is a student of Roger Bacon, a real life Franciscan friar and philosopher who, inspired by Islamic scientists, is credited with being one of the earliest European advocates of the "scientific method." This empiricism is evident in William's discussions with Adso about events in the corpse-strewn abbey. What he tries to impress upon his young charge is the importance of being able to hold several, maybe contradictory, "truths" in one's head simultaneously. In wrestling with the mystery of what is behind the killings, William behaves consistently with his approach to learning and knowledge. He uses the evidence to develop a multitude of competing hypotheses and is comfortable pursuing these in parallel, until some further piece of evidence suggests additions or alterations to this collection. By imagining many possibilities he becomes "the slave of none." The only problem with this is that, meanwhile, monks keep dropping dead.

This suggests several possible lessons for the mentor:

- In order to help our learners discover new knowledge and grapple with complex problems, we must be prepared to accept ambiguity and competing possibilities without rushing to "correct" answers. Very often, the mentor will be just as much out of their depth, and there is no harm in admitting this and discovering new ideas together.
- Part of our role may be seen as helping to create alternative options and possibilities, just as another part of our role is to help people prioritize, narrow down and focus. (There's a nice ambiguity for us to practice living with!)
- One of the things we bring to our learners is "process knowledge," an understanding of how one can use enquiry and reflection to mentor oneself. Should we be acting as role models in demonstrating how continuous learning is best served by open-minded questioning and consideration of multiple possibilities?
- However, all this exploration and weighing and hypothesizing must be balanced with the learner's need to take action to address their goals. Building knowledge and making sense of things can never be a substitute for action, because action is a crucial part of the learning cycle.

Let us try to illustrate this last point further. By the end of the story, with William's encouragement, Adso is beginning to apply William's process to his own thinking. He even unwittingly uncovers part of the solution to the code which unlocks the door into a secret part of the library. But the change in Adso that is brought about through his experiences with Willliam of Baskerville goes deeper than this. In his dream, towards the end of the tale, we are shown the extent to which his time with William has led Adso to question all his previous assumptions about truth, knowledge and religious orthodoxy, and how this has turned his world upside down. At its most extreme then, the potential dangers of William's world view are apparent:

- By rejecting anything as true, we can generate cynicism
- By multiplying options and possibilities, we can generate confusion
- Cynicism and confusion lead to inaction, and without action and experimentation the familiar learning cycle is broken
- The result is paralysis and stagnation

WISE GUYS – THE DOWNSIDE OF AMBIGUITY

This raises an interesting question for the mentor. What is our responsibility towards the learner if we choose to reject universal truth and historical solutions in favour of ambiguity, enquiry and continuous learning? The glib answer to this conundrum is, of course, that we hold these two contradictory ideas in our head at once and thereby become the "slave" of neither. But the danger is that, in a world where knowledge and truth are relative, it may be possible to prove nothing, but it's just as easy to justify anything.

Which brings us to the morally ambiguous world of *The Sopranos*. For the uninitiated (shame on you!), *The Sopranos* is an award-winning television drama series, created by David Chase, about Tony Soprano, a fictional New Jersey-based mafia boss, his family and his "family." As Tony (played by James Gandolfini) battles with establishing and defending his criminal empire, he is threatened by competing bosses, by the FBI, by informants within his own "crew," and sometimes by the sheer brutal incompetence of his lieutenants and minions. In this regard, he is (hopefully) not much like you or me. But he is also troubled by conflicts within his own family (Carmela, his wife, Meadow, his daughter, and Anthony Jr., his son), beset by doubts about how to handle relationships with his wife and children, and frequently unhappy and racked with anxiety about keeping "all the balls in the air": a demanding job, a family to support, elderly dependent relatives, and lazy, scheming or over-zealous colleagues. In this respect, he is perhaps easier to identify with. His efforts to make sense of what all this means and to find the right course of action amid all these conflicts brings on anxiety attacks which cause him to seek the continuing help of a psychiatrist, Jennifer Melfi. We find ourselves identifying with his dilemmas and self-doubt, despite the fact that we routinely witness him taking part in robbery, extortion, casual marital infidelity, savage assaults and murder. As an exercise in managing ambiguity, this story takes some beating (as do many of its characters).

In exploring further the themes we have uncovered in *The Name of the Rose*, we will focus here on the relationship between Tony Soprano and Jennifer Melfi (played by Lorraine Bracco). Obviously, this is a therapeutic rather than a mentoring relationship. Moreover, this partnership has the added complication of a certain sexual attraction on both sides. Tony fantasizes about Dr. Melfi, and there are hints that, despite her frequent disgust, she is oddly attracted to him. These feelings are never consummated (not for want of Tony trying), and we shall choose to ignore them here. But Tony and Dr. Melfi encounter interesting questions about the nature of all one-to-one helping relationships, particularly when it comes to the use of knowledge and the challenges of relativism.

ALL INSIGHT AND NO ACTION

Dr. Melfi agrees to help Tony, despite his open acknowledgement of his "profession." We presume this is because she sees her role as being there to help, rather than to judge, perhaps because she holds out some possibly naïve hope of making him a better person, but maybe also, we suspect, because she is intrigued and not a little excited by the prospect of treating a mob boss. Melfi does not approve of Tony's life and frequently makes no effort to hide this judgement. Nevertheless, the therapy continues, exploring Tony's relationship with his manipulative and murderous mother, Livia, his struggles with his own children, and the approaching dispersal of his family, (symbolized famously by the ducks leaving his swimming pool).[3]

On the face of it, Tony's relationship with Jennifer Melfi has succeeded in helping him to develop considerable insight, into his own motivations, his relationships, especially with his mother, and the origins of his anxiety attacks. Furthermore, as a result of the sessions he has learned more about the whole process of psychological enquiry. He is better educated about how to make sense of behavior and its causes. He has become more therapy-literate. As mentors, we might well count as a resounding success a relationship where such insight and appreciation of the process of learning and personal change has been achieved by the learner.

But here is the problem. After four years' of therapy, we can be forgiven for concluding that Tony has not really changed at all. He remains to the end a murderous and vicious gangster. How should we respond to this? Who is the judge of what constitutes transition or personal growth? Had Jennifer Melfi been hired as Tony's mentor rather than as his psychotherapist, would he have viewed his increased repertoire of "leadership and management strategies" as a successful outcome? Well probably not. On balance, there is little evidence that even Tony would regard these relatively meagre rewards for four years of "learning dialogue" as representing good value for money. What has been gained from the insight he has achieved? The lesson for us as mentors seems clear enough:

- Knowledge and insight is less important than what you do with it.
- Knowledge and insight does not in itself produce change. It is only the beginning of a learner's journey, not the end.

This idea – what they termed the "knowing-doing gap" – was studied in depth by Pfeffer and Sutton in their book of the same name.[4] The danger it presents is that organizations as well as individuals routinely fail to *apply* their knowledge, and that it is only by implementation that knowledge is built, maintained and transferred successfully. Keeping it locked in libraries, spending hours discussing it in meetings (or mentoring sessions), or having it inserted into you via further and higher education programmes does not result in us getting the value from what we know, nor in us developing it further. Know-how, they argue, has to be applied appropriately within a specific context in order to have relevance. Knowledge management is not therefore about storage or memory, but about constant application, experimentation, action and learning. Any approach that sees knowledge as fixed and established will only limit an organization's or an individual's capacity to grow and adapt. As mentors, therefore, our focus must be at least as much on how the learner is going to take action and apply learning as it is on the process of insight and knowledge creation. But are we sure this is reflected in our practice?

> MENTEE: The most amazing mentoring session I ever had was with a guy who helped me explore my self-destructive tendency to provoke and alienate my senior male colleagues in the organization. In encouraging me to talk about my family background, he helped me to realize that my rebellious and fractious relationship with my father was somehow triggering this negative attitude to male authority figures....
> MENTOR: Fascinating stuff....So what did you do about this?
> MENTEE: Sorry...How do you mean?"

How large does the process of turning insight into action really loom in our mentoring sessions?

> MENTOR: If I'm honest, I typically spend most of the session helping the client explore the issues, generate possibilities and hypotheses, and draw some useful conclusions about what will move them further towards their goals, whatever they may be. I certainly don't neglect the action planning, and I absolutely understand the way the learning cycle works, but I suppose I devote maybe 10–20%, at most, of our time in a session to the detail of what action the client will take and when.

There is little doubt that the process of generating insight is the "sexy" part of the mentoring dialogue. It is the part that many mentor "war stories" seem to dwell upon. By comparison, the often repetitive and frustrating grind of helping someone to take action and undergo changes in behavior which they find difficult or downright scary, can appear distinctly less clever and exciting[5]. But if we see the turning of insight and knowledge into action and change as not only more important, but possibly more difficult, then it is worth reflecting on where we currently place our time and effort. We explore this topic of personal change further in Chapter Five.

So, is it simply about sharing and co-creating knowledge, then turning it into action, or is there more to it than that?

CREATING YOUR OWN REALITY

In *The Matrix*, the Wachowski brothers' film about a nightmare future in which the world is run by machines, an office "drone" and secret superhacker, called Thomas Anderson (played by Keanu Reeves) is discovered and mentored by Morpheus (Laurence Fishburne), the leader of an underground resistance movement. Unlike the rest of humanity, Morpheus and his comrades know that the world humanity "sees" is actually an elaborate computer simulation, and we are all, in fact, prisoners of the machines, trapped in a world laid waste, and floating naked, without hair or eyebrows, in little pods full of jelly, wired up to a massive computer which simulates the "normal" world we would all recognize. Morpheus and co. have escaped from their pods, grown back their hair and eyebrows (well, OK not Laurence Fishburne), and found a way of plugging themselves into the simulation and escaping it when they like. In the simulation, they are chased by "agents" who look like people and can kill them, even though it's a simulation (yes, I know), and in the real world they're chased by machines which can either kill them, or, I guess, put them back in the jelly. Morpheus believes Thomas Anderson to be Neo, "the One," a kind of messiah figure whose powers will transcend the capabilities of normal mortals and allow the agents and machines to be defeated. (His name is, of course, an anagram of "one." It's not difficult, but then again this is not *University Challenge*.)

As well as being very cool indeed, Morpheus is actually a more skilful mentor than many of those we find portrayed in film and television. At their first meeting, he displays a notable degree of humility, and chooses to ask lots of questions of Thomas, rather than launch immediately into explanations and plot exposition. He offers him a choice as to whether he wants to remain in the world of comfortable illusion, or be exposed to the true predicament of humanity, and even when training Thomas in the martial arts which are a key feature of the film, he asks him questions about how he beat him, and what assumptions he is making about the difference his muscles will make in a simulated world. There can be no doubt that Morpheus introduces his learner to a whole new world view. (This alternative reality also explains how Morpheus is able to engage in prolonged bouts of martial arts whilst wearing pince-nez sunglasses.)

We began this chapter examining how we develop knowledge in the context of multiple truths, alternative realities and different perspectives, and certainly in *The Matrix* we have a vivid representation of how fragile and unreliable any one version of truth and reality can be. But it is the connection between knowing and doing which is what most concerns us here.

ONLY BELIEVE...

Thomas's initial training in the hand-to-hand combat techniques he will need to defeat the machines (eh?) consists of being "plugged into" computer programs, which download all the necessary know-how into his brain via a hole in the back of his head. As a metaphor for a mechanistic view of skills and knowledge development, it is hard to beat. Those managers in organizations who still believe, despite copious amounts of evidence to the contrary, that sending people on courses will somehow miraculously transform their abilities and behavior, would probably love to get hold of this technology and start drilling holes in the back of all their employees' heads tomorrow. But, to its credit, *The Matrix* suggests a slightly more sophisticated model.

For Thomas's "technical" knowledge does not really bear fruit, in terms of actually winning these eye-popping fights, until he stops thinking and starts believing and doing it for real. Morpheus tells him to stop *thinking* he is faster and "know" he is, to stop *trying* to hit him and hit him. Thomas loses quite badly several times in his clashes with the agents, before he begins to really believe in his identity as Neo, the "one" and at this point his martial arts skills, and other powers increase exponentially. Admittedly, we can see this as mere wish-fulfilment hokum, the kind of "if you believe it you can do it" generalization that peppers a lot of the underdog/evil-doer clashes that film-makers love so much. But beneath the bland, pseudo-psychology lies an interesting premise.

If we take the view that truth, reality, knowledge, whatever, is not a consistent set of constructs which exists outside ourselves and can be accessed objectively in the same way by everyone, then what really starts to matter is how we personally frame events and respond to them. If the world largely exists inside our own head, as the result of electrical signals interpreted by our brain, and therefore interpreted differently by different people, then we are all living in "the matrix" to a degree. OK, we might not go as far as to say we can entirely create our own reality, and, say, fly in the air, as Neo eventually does, but it does suggest that what we believe and what we do, as a result, can have at least as big an impact on our reality as what we think we know. So, the interpretation we place on events, and therefore how we respond to them, allows us, to a degree, to create our own "truth," our own "reality."

> MENTOR: Howard was struggling with getting used to his new boss. He'd spent the last ten years working for a highly sociable and easy-going guy, who knew all his staff well, took an interest in their personal lives, and laughed and joked with them frequently. He was the kind

of person who was blessed with highly-developed social skills and naturally made everyone feel important and at ease.

His new boss, Steve, a younger bloke, kept himself to himself, only seemed interested in the job, and confined his communication to brief (and slightly cryptic) comments. Howard had convinced himself that Steve had taken a dislike to him and had a low opinion of his abilities. He had become paranoid about being eased out in the next reorganization.

As his mentor, I challenged him to think of critical incidents involving Steve, and suggested alternative interpretations of events. I asked Howard to put himself in Steve's shoes. Could it be that Steve was actually a bit scared himself in a new job, struggling with his lack of relationship-building skills and yet desperately wanting to make a mark. What if he wasn't the enemy? What if he actually needed help from Howard to complement his own skills and develop ways of being more effective as a boss? What if Howard was at his most confident and secure? How might he help Steve to do his job better?

That got us talking about lots of things Howard could do, around asking for feedback, reporting back to Steve in a way he would value, helping smooth the relationship between Steve, other members of his team and senior colleagues. Eventually, this became a self-fulfilling prophesy. As Steve came to appreciate Howard's contribution, and take advantage of what he could learn from him, their relationship strengthened and Steve was much more open.

I've still no idea the extent to which Howard's initial paranoia was justified, but, in a way, it didn't really matter.

This is the "fake it till you make it" school of thought, which reverses the view of knowledge held by the owners of our mediaeval library. In their world, we acquire the one true knowledge which causes us to act in a way that defines who we are.[6] In the world of "the matrix" we can choose to believe in another version of who we are, allowing us to act in way which creates a *new* truth or piece of knowledge.

Thomas Anderson enters his final battle of the film to rescue his new comrades, actually believing that Morpheus has been mistaken in identifying him as the saviour, because the "oracle," an elderly African-American lady in housecoat and slippers, has told him this. She also tells him that Morpheus is so convinced he is "the One" that he will sacrifice his life to save him. Consequently, Thomas feels obliged to re-enter "the matrix," even though he "knows" that he hasn't the power to conquer the agents. It is only after his defeat of Agent Smith in the subway that Morpheus tells Neo that there is a difference between "knowing the path" and "walking the path," and that the oracle has told him only what he needed to hear. In other words, it would not be enough for Thomas to be told that he was "the One'; he needed to believe this for himself, and that could only happen as a result of him going back into the matrix to try and save Morpheus. Because this is how he would eventually apply his skills and knowledge in a way that would convince him of his powers and transform him into Neo.

SO, WHAT CAN WE LEARN....?

At this point, before we lose our own grip on reality, it may be helpful to sum up where this all gets us:

- We can view knowledge and truth as relative and ever-changing, depending on circumstance, perspective etc.
- Your knowledge, or version of the truth may therefore be different from mine, but no less valid.
- If this is so, we are best served by maintaining a state of "not knowing," of continuous learning and enquiry, in order to keep building our knowledge. This means accepting ambiguity and multiple "truths."
- We can only do this by sharing and applying what we know, subjecting it to experimentation and interpretation in order to create new knowledge.
- But experimentation implies action, and part of this learning cycle has to be action, because insight alone is useless to us and results in nothing changing.
- Because, to a degree, we create our own truth in the way we interpret the world and events within it, we can choose an interpretation which enables us to act in a way that creates a new truth, a new "knowledge."

How is all this relevant to us, as mentors? Well, in more ways than we might at first have thought. For example:

- We can accept ambiguities and multiple interpretations of the world and encourage our learners to do likewise.
- We can provide alternative perspectives and suggest new ways of seeing.
- We can help to generate multiple possibilities and options in addressing dilemmas and issues.
- We can help our learners to understand better the process of learning and building knowledge via such means, in order that they might become more self-sufficient in their own continuous learning.
- However, we must also help learners to focus and prioritize when appropriate.

- Also we must avoid "paralysis by analysis" and never forget the overriding importance of action and doing something with this insight and knowledge. Without action, change is impossible.
- Finally, one way of achieving such change may be by adjusting our beliefs and assumptions to reflect a different reality and then acting in accordance with that anyway.

REFERENCES

[1]Alred, G., & Garvey, R. (2000). Learning to Produce Knowledge – the Contribution of Mentoring. *Mentoring & Tutoring, 8*(3).

[2]Daloz, L. (1999). *Mentor,* San Francisco, CA: Jossey-Bass.

[3]Greene, R., & Vernezze, P. (Eds.), (2004). *The Sopranos and Philosophy,* Chicago: Open Court.

[4]Pfeffer, J., & Sutton, R.I. (2000). *The Knowing-doing Gap: How Smart Companies Turn Knowledge Into Action,* Boston: Harvard Business Press.

[5]Smail, D. (1987). *Taking Care, An Alternative to Therapy,* London: J.M Dent & Sons Ltd.

[6]Taylor, D. (2007). *The Naked Coach,* Chichester, UK: Capstone.

Television, Films and Books

Arnaud, J.-J. (Director). (1986). *The Name of the Rose* [Motion picture]. France/Italy/W. Germany: Neue Constantin Film. (From the novel by Umberto Eco (1983), published by Harcourt.)

Chase, D. (Producer). (1986). *The Sopranos* [Television series]. New York: HBO. (Ran from 1999 to 2007.)

Wachowski, A, & Wachowski, L. (1999). *The Matrix* [Motion picture]. Melbourne, Australia: Village Roadshow Pictures, US.

CHAPTER 3

VAMPIRES, HUSTLERS AND TOUGH LOVE

The Use and Abuse of Power and Trust

INTERVIEW WITH THE VAMPIRE

In *Interview with the Vampire*, the film based on the best-selling novel by Anne Rice, the story of Lestat and Louis, played somewhat controversially at the time by Tom Cruise and Brad Pitt respectively, is recounted in flashback to an eager journalist (played by Christian Slater), who describes himself as a "collector of lives." The story of Louis's relationship with the vampire Lestat begins in 1791 in New Orleans and continues across the centuries (and the continents) to present day San Francisco. In the course of their travels, they "adopt" Claudia, a young girl they have made one of their own kind, and for a while live like a sort of family (albeit a seriously dysfunctional one). Louis and Claudia eventually escape from Lestat and flee to nineteenth century Paris, where they hook up with some "old world" vampires. These, led by Armand (Antonio Banderas), run a bizarre, post-modern theatre, in which they act out being vampires for their (presumably) innocent audience, whilst actually sucking people's blood for real on stage.

Is there anything here that looks remotely like mentoring? Well, leaving aside for a moment the fact that Lestat is one of the "undead"; a vampire who feeds off the blood of his innocent victims, the partnership of Louis and Lestat does have several of the hallmarks of a mentoring relationship. Lestat first meets Louis at a crisis point in his life. Louis, a plantation owner, has lost all his family to disease, and as a consequence has lost his own will to live. Lestat helps Louis to make a major transition in his life, in fact a transition he could never have imagined, to a new "life" of immortality. Furthermore, Lestat offers Louis a choice. He does not turn him into a vampire against his will, as did the vampire who made *him*, but rather he allows Louis to choose. (I should point out the other option was probably death, so not much of a choice really, except of course that death is what Louis had been longing for.)

Undoubtedly, in inducting Louis into the world of vampires Lestat, like any mentor, shows Louis the ropes (and the coffins, and the metal fingernails for slitting people's throats). He supports Louis in making the "difficult" physical transition to being undead and feeding on blood, helpfully showing him for example how small animals can substitute for humans when circumstances demand (on long sea voyages apparently). Ultimately, their acquaintance lasts for 200 years (and counting), probably some sort of a record for a mentoring partnership.

So what relevance can such a fantastic tale have for us in the kind of mentoring relationships we know? Well crucially this is a story of *manipulation*. After all, it's all about vampires, not the most subtle metaphor for a parasitic relationship.

THE MANIPULATIVE MENTOR 1 – PLAYING GOD

As mentors, we must tread what is sometimes a narrow path between helping and interfering, between enabling and control. Some mentors can misunderstand their role. Poor training, lack of self-awareness or questionable motives can lead mentors to stray from this path and behave in ways not so very different from Lestat. Not that they start sleeping in coffins during the day, or biting people's necks, but they may be tempted to feel that they alone have the "answers." They can see their role as "putting the learner straight" and providing solutions to their problems, dispensing the wisdom they have gained from long years of experience. They play mind games with their learners, using the power they bring into the relationship as a result of being the mentor, the voice of experience and the "elder statesman" to exercise influence over the learner and their decisions, because it flatters their ego to do it. They seek to mould people in their own image, to instil their own knowledge, attitudes and behavior into the learner.[1] In short, they play God.

MENTOR: When I mentor Jill, I find a part of me dreading the endless, wandering narrative of her life. I'm torn between the desire to be a good listener and the urge take control and strategize more, if only to get her to a decision, some kind of learning point. I sincerely want her to be getting value for money from this process. But then that can smack a bit of knowing what's good for her. A very dangerous road....

Lestat plays God, not only in giving others' immortality, but also in trying to create more vampires in his own image, ruthless predators feeding happily on the lives of innocent humans. He is enraged by Louis' moral objections to taking human life, and constantly badgers and tempts him into becoming as remorseless a killer as he is. A tendency to "bully" the learner in a direction they do not feel committed to themselves – what might be termed harassment – has been identified in previous research as one of the hallmarks of dysfunctional mentoring.[2] We suspect Lestat's only real motive in answering Louis's desperate prayers is actually a selfish one: to give himself a like-minded companion to share the loneliness of eternity. He turns Claudia, the little girl, into a vampire partly to bait Louis, but perhaps also because he wants someone as voracious and amoral as himself for company. He is proud of Claudia's lust for killing, as if she were his own infant prodigy. When Claudia asks him how he made her a vampire, he declines to tell her, only saying that it was in his power to do so. It is instructive to note the contrast with Louis's other mentor in the story, Armand, the world's oldest vampire, who welcomes Louis's questions and the opportunity to share knowledge.

THE ETERNAL CHILD – MENTORING AND DEPENDENCY

It is easy to dismiss all this as the province of "toxic mentors." But even as competent, well-trained mentors, in it for all the right reasons, we can still stray. We know that our role is to help the learner reflect on experience, explore and analyze options and discover their own solutions by supporting, and challenging, within a partnership based on mutual respect and acceptance. However, we want to help, and this most laudable of motives can be our undoing. We all find it hard to see someone struggle, and the same zeal that makes us mentors in the first place can make us mistake *our* desire to teach, change or rescue someone for *their* own need to reflect and learn. Sometimes we neglect the very necessary process of exploration and reflection in order to focus too quickly on a problem we think we have an answer to. Most of us have spent our lives in jobs which actively encourage and reward us for "fixing" things, solving problems, putting things right, and doing it as quickly as possible. Small wonder then that, as mentors, we sometimes find ourselves fighting a very natural urge to "sort out" the lives of others. Whether our intent is malicious and selfish or not, the result is often the same: dependency on the part of the learner.

Which brings us to perhaps the most powerful image in *Interview with the Vampire*. Claudia (played in the film by a young, and mesmerizing, Kirsten Dunst) is turned into a vampire against her will by Lestat, who exploits Louis's remorse over attacking her and possibly letting her die, to add her to the "family." In doing so, he gives her eternal life. She becomes immortal, but she can never grow old, condemned to have the mind of a grown woman in the body of a child. Lestat continues to buy her dolls long after she has grown out of them, and he treats Claudia herself like a doll, taking pleasure in dressing her up in pretty clothes and revelling in a sense of "ownership."

In this unsettling image of a woman with adult appetites spending eternity in the body of a ghostly, pale doll-child, we have one of the most powerful metaphors of manipulation and dependency one can imagine.

THE MANIPULATIVE MENTOR 2 –
DECEPTION AND COLLUSION

In the Martin Scorsese film *The Color of Money*, a younger and extravagantly coiffed Tom Cruise is this time on the receiving end of a less-than-perfect mentoring relationship. We are twenty-five years on from the time of *The Hustler* and Paul Newman reprises the role of "Fast Eddie" Felson that he played in the earlier film. Now a moderately successful liquor salesman, Eddie "discovers" Vincent Lauria (Tom Cruise), a talented, but immature pool player, and sets out to mentor him.

As in *Vampire* this is a mentoring relationship based on manipulation. After all, Eddie is the consummate hustler. Finding people's weaknesses and using this insight to deceive and manipulate them is his stock in trade. What he admires most in Vincent is his ability to look like a "flake." In a world where hiding one's abilities and intentions is key, it's a gift as important as the pool-playing itself. (Of course, this may be a nuance lost on the audience who, on seeing a leather-clad, pompadour-headed Tom Cruise with Paul Newman in sharkskin suit and oversized shades, would pretty unanimously assume they were professional hustlers! Having said that, this was, of course, the Eighties.)

Again, research tells us that, along with harassment and submissiveness, deception is a third characteristic of dysfunctional mentoring.[2] From the start Eddie persuades Vincent to go on the road with him by planting fears in his mind about his girlfriend, Carmen, getting bored with him and the small-time life he leads. Later, Eddie colludes with Carmen in order to manoeuvre Vincent into doing what *he* wants. If such Machiavellian goings-on seem a long way from the mentoring *you* practice, just think of the multiple relationships mentors have to manage, with line managers, partners (business and otherwise), scheme administrators and senior management sponsors. What sort of triangulation can mentors sometimes find themselves seduced into, if they are not careful, by bosses or organizations sponsoring the process?

When Vincent takes pity on an old-timer with a tracheotomy and refuses to hustle him, Eddie deliberately allows his protégé to get attacked and beaten up to teach him that no-one deserves mercy, and then "rescues" him from the mob before they can do too much damage. In this way he cleverly cements his position, both as expert who is always to be obeyed and supportive father-figure. Most experienced mentors will recognize the potential in any relationship for the learner to play the "victim," even if unwittingly, and will equally acknowledge the often seductive attraction of casting oneself as "rescuer," maybe as the result of a misplaced desire to help. We may not set out to create this dynamic, as Eddie does, but we should not underestimate the self-control required by the mentor to resist this "shadow side."[3] Learners can be inclined to seek more directive intervention deliberately, as it relieves them of the burden of thinking for themselves (and/or taking responsibility for the outcome). It is something most experienced mentors will recognize, and something they know they must be constantly alert to. The usual result, as with playing God, is increased dependency.

But what other dimensions of manipulative mentoring are portrayed in *The Color of Money*, and what questions do they raise for us as practising mentors?

WHOSE SIDE ARE YOU ON? – CONFLICTS AND AUTHENTICITY

First of all Eddie is fatally compromised by a conflict of interest. Since as Vincent's "stakehorse" he takes 60% of everything Vincent wins, it is impossible for him to be objective and follow his learner's agenda and best interests. The conflicts we need to be alert to are unlikely to be quite this obvious. Are we being given one agenda by our learner and another by the organization which may be employing us or paying the bill? How involved can we afford to become in the success of the small business we are mentoring? Does our historic loyalty and relationship with the boss inhibit our ability to mentor the subordinate they have a problematic relationship with? Are we avoiding challenging our learner about some aspect of their behavior because we fear it may prematurely end our work together and possibly a source of income?

Secondly, Eddie is actively teaching Vincent to lose his authenticity. Vincent is a naturally enthusiastic player who loves to show off his skills. In a memorable scene he grandstands shamelessly whilst beating Moselle to the tune of *Werewolves of London*. But Eddie shows him how to dissemble and keep his talent under wraps until big money is at stake. Of course, in the context of becoming a successful hustler and making some substantial sums of money, Eddie's help "works." Towards the end of the film Vincent seems pretty pleased at the money he has made while on the road without Eddie, so we assume this has, in some way, fulfilled a goal of his. And yet we are left feeling uncomfortable. From a brash, but talented and natural young sportsperson Vincent has become a cynical, mercenary and manipulative con man. Should our sensibility as mentors, who strive to help people become more authentically themselves, be offended by this outcome, regardless of its financial success? Maybe so. As mentors, we have a responsibility to encourage authenticity on the part of the learner, and therefore an obligation to role model this behavior ourselves. But do we always live up to this?

> MENTOR: I worry that I'm being dishonest with Anil, not really myself, sitting here pretending to be patient when I'm secretly tearing my hair out. Should I voice my feelings? Is our relationship strong enough for me to share the frustration I'm experiencing? We've met a few times now, but I'm not sure I've got to know the real him, what makes him tick....or that he has done so with me really....

THE PARASITIC MENTOR – LIVING YOUR LIFE FOR YOU

Finally, Eddie illustrates perfectly one of the most dangerous traps lying in wait for the unaware mentor: that of living vicariously through your learner. At first, Eddie's career as a professional pool player seems over. He relates the story of how he had the "screws" put on him 25 years before. He mourns that his career was "over before it started." One interpretation of his partnership with Vincent is that he sees an opportunity to recapture past excitement and glory through the younger man. He persuades him to recreate his own journey, to the extent of playing the same pool halls, even though the world has changed in 25 years and some are now, like Eddie, in mothballs. Newly inspired by this taste of his youth, Eddie rediscovers his "mojo" and starts winning, capping it all with a win over his former pupil at the Atlantic City tournament, only to discover crushingly that Vincent has thrown the match deliberately in order to win a side bet. When Eddie forfeits his next match in order to informally play Vincent, it is because he knows Vincent has become the one to beat. The tables have turned (no pun intended). It is now Eddie who wants only to win and prove he is the best, and Vincent who follows the money.

Let us be perfectly clear. There is nothing whatsoever wrong with the mentor learning from the relationship, gaining new perspectives, growing their own understanding and benefiting from insights that might prompt small changes or even seismic shifts in their own lives. But this is about mutuality and exchange, not exploitation of one party to the benefit of the other. What is crucial here is the orientation of the mentor. Are they primarily focused on helping their learner, or is their primary motivation gaining or regaining some outcome of their own?

> MENTOR: It's like Jackie and I have skipped a step and, because of our common backgrounds in sales and marketing, dived into the issues and strategies. I wonder whether I'm actually enjoying the chance to develop marketing strategy again, rather than focusing on helping her. Having a clear brief that I'm here to help her make more of a strategic impact probably isn't helping....

In this case, you are left with the feeling that Vincent is right when he accuses Eddie of "using" him. Whether we see Eddie as a grifter who "accidentally" rediscovers his love of the sport and will to win, or whether we see the relationship with Vincent as a deliberate ploy to get himself back in the game, there can be no doubt that he was putting his own interests first and Vincent was something of a pawn in all this. It's much harder to interpret this as a two-way learning alliance from which both parties benefit and learn, largely because that never seems to be the intent. When Eddie cuts Vincent loose to go out on his own with a bit of seed money, we could view this as him doing what a good mentor should. That is, he is encouraging self-reliance once it is clear there is no further learning in the partnership, and maybe because he regrets the seedy world he has dragged Vincent into. Alternatively, we might say, having just been taken for a patsy by Amos (Forrest Whittaker), he is angry and anxious to get on with his own comeback.

Listen to this "mentor"... Whose interests is he really focused on?

> MENTOR: ..it's ever so complimentary. It's so rewarding when people just get on and do things because they recognize that's probably the right way of doing it.....that there's somebody here with a lot more ideas than they've got....or, sorry, not more ideas, but more experience than they have.......I guess what I've got out of it is a confidence or a need to go back into business...[3]

And what is his learner's take on it all?

MENTEE: You know, it was a bit like talking to my Dad really....But I wouldn't say I learned anything from him....I felt like I was doing it for him and not for me, because I was kind of going in a direction I didn't want to be going in...[3]

IT'S THE RELATIONSHIP, STUPID...

In research by the U.K. Chartered Institute of Personnel and Development into coaching in organizations, a key conclusion was that the quality of the coaching relationship is not just important, but the "single most important" factor determining success in coaching.[4] Other research and many esteemed writers and commentators in the mentoring field would readily support the same assertion for mentoring.[5] Building trust and managing the power dynamics within a one-to-one helping relationship quite rightly exercises the mind of any conscientious mentor who is looking to get better at what they do.

So what is it about our relationships with learners which builds and maintains this trust? What is it mentors do to develop the kind of relationship within which we both feel safe enough to disclose important feelings, frustrations, fears and joys, without worrying that we will make fools of ourselves or mortally offend the other person? Equally importantly, what are the bear traps waiting out there to snare the unwitting mentor, and maybe pull them over that line that divides help and learning from coercion and manipulation?

So far we have focused on mentoring relationships which have been undermined by problems of:

- *Control* – The desire, whether calculated or not, to control the learner, to mould them according to our values and standards, to create them in our image
- *Concern* – A concern primarily for oneself or for a particular goal, not for the individual learner. Often manifesting itself in living vicariously through another in order to recapture your own self-esteem
- *Intervention* – An emphasis on "fixing," or changing people, rather than enabling them to pursue their own development
- *Agenda* – The mistaken assumption that the mentor knows best and has a major contribution to the learner's goals
- *Trust* – In such relationships trust is either misplaced or missing altogether

But where can we look to find more positive examples of the way a true learning partnership should be managed?

GOOD WILL HUNTING

In *Good Will Hunting*, we are introduced to Will Hunting, a young man from the wrong side of the tracks, damaged by past abuse, and living a blue-collar existence with his buddies in South Boston. But Will is no ordinary "southie." He is possessed of a genius for learning and can solve math problems that are beyond the capabilities of professors at MIT.

Much of the film focuses on Will's encounters with his therapist, Sean, played by a hirsute and unkempt Robin Williams. Quite clearly, Sean is a psychiatrist and, as with Dr. Melfi and Tony Soprano, this is a therapeutic relationship. Sean is helping Will come to terms with childhood abuse and overcome the fear of abandonment and the defensiveness this has led to. However, much more of their dialogue and the mutual learning it leads to has to do with helping Will to grow up, decide how he wants to make use of his undoubted gifts, and take responsibility for his life choices. This has much more in common with mentoring and there are several issues of interest here to anyone fulfilling a mentoring role.

RAPPORT-BUILDING – TECHNIQUE VERSUS TRUST

When we first encounter Sean, significantly enough, he is talking to his community college class about trust and rapport in the helping relationship. This will be the major challenge in his work with Will. To begin with, the signs are not good. Will is being forced to see a therapist as a condition of his release from a custodial sentence (for attacking a police officer) into the care of Gerry, the prize-winning math professor at MIT who has spotted Will's talent. He has already been through five other therapists, some of whom even we the audience recognize as pompous, out to "fix" him and generally exploiting their "superior" knowledge and power. Although he cuts them down to size by precociously anticipating and ridiculing their diagnoses and treatments, still, we sense that Will has developed a negative impression of therapists as a result of this experience, and, one assumes, his history of institutionalization. In fact, when first offered the get-out-of-jail deal by Gerry, he says yes to spending all day on math problems and no to therapy. This is some measure of his distaste for that kind of help, well-meaning or otherwise.

> Jennifer was asked to provide executive mentoring to Kurt, a senior civil servant. She had been engaged by Kurt's boss, Caroline, someone she knew from her former career in a large corporate. Having recently moved into a new

role, Caroline had inherited Kurt, who came to her with a reputation for being somewhat cautious and bureaucratic. Caroline's leadership style was founded on delegating as much responsibility as practicable and making individuals accountable. Anxious to draw some lines in the sand at the start of her new "regime," she had made it clear to Kurt that his continued role in the team depended on him accepting some mentoring to help him make the transition to the new style of management. Jennifer, faced with a somewhat reluctant learner who felt he'd been left with little choice but to take part, had to work very hard to establish anything resembling trust and rapport.

Faced with a situation like this, many mentors have an easy solution. They simply refuse to get involved because the prospects for success are so reduced. However, this is only an extreme example of a more common phenomenon. Learners often feel forced into mentoring relationships, some overtly by organizational pressures and expectations, others more subtly by the sense that they must change or develop in some way to achieve their goals or become the person they want to be. In order to establish a "safe space" in which someone is comfortable engaging in an open and honest learning dialogue, the mentor must first earn the right, the permission, to play this role.[6]

So, by the time he has his first meeting with Sean, Will is a reluctant "client" with a deep-seated contempt for the therapist's role. Consequently it is pretty much doomed from the start. Here is our first lesson then. All the interpersonal skills and rapport-building techniques in the world will not cut it if there is no trust in the relationship. Sean manfully employs his armory of rapport-building approaches, as might we. This covers an increasingly desperate range of topics: the fact that both hail from the poor South side of Boston; Will's interest in books; and their shared experience of weight-lifting. Furthermore, all of this is pursued by a cuddly, non-threatening guy with a lumpy cardigan and a winning sense of humour. But Will remains resolutely defensive and uncooperative, and the conversation rapidly descends into a verbal sparring match to see who can get the most references and allusions. The fact that Sean's attempts to build rapport are so transparent is not itself a problem. It is that the technique is doomed until Sean has won Will's trust and earned the right to start building a relationship.

The first meeting ends, none too auspiciously with Will goading Sean about his lack of direction and continuing obsession with his dead wife, and Sean losing his temper and pinning his learner to the wall. Not really the sort of thing we should emulate, however much we might sometimes feel like it. In meeting two, on a park bench, Sean challenges Will's apparent air of self-possession by offering the insight that Will uses his precocious knowledge as a weapon to keep people at a distance, because he is scared of engaging with the world. This is a high risk strategy on Sean's part, which

seems to work for a couple of reasons. One is that the observation is probably pretty accurate and gains some tacit and grudging admiration from
Will. The other is that in highlighting the difference between Will's book
learning and real-life experience, Sean actually reveals a lot about himself
and his critical experiences, (love for his wife, losing friends in Vietnam and
so on). Sean successfully continues this tactic in future meetings, talking
about his late wife's "farting" for example. Although meeting three is spent
in complete silence, as Will is still not ready to trust anyone outside his small
circle of close friends, eventually Sean's readiness to be open and make
himself vulnerable wins through. He is not only winning Will's trust but
effectively role-modelling the kind of behavior Will is increasingly going to
have to adopt in order to build his own relationships, with the Harvard Law
student, Skyler, for example (played by Minnie Driver).

All this raises an interesting question about rapport-building skills and
technique. The kind of productive dialogue on which mentoring is built is
held together by the skilful use of active listening, questioning, reflecting,
summarizing, and all the rest. But we can see from Sean's experience that
on their own they do not make for a mutually trusting relationship. We
might even go so far as to say that interpersonal skills in this context are
something of a "hygiene factor."[7] In other words, a good mentor needs a
degree of expertise in this field in order to build trust and conduct a constructive dialogue, but increasingly slick use of technique does not generally lead to greater and greater trust or better and better dialogue. Think of
public figures you know who appear well-trained in the art of communication and influencing. Does it make you trust them?

Inevitably there is a tension here. We use skills and techniques to build
relationships, but technique is also inextricably linked in our minds with
manipulation. Suddenly we're back to vampires and hustlers again.

CARING, HUMOUR AND AUTHENTICITY

In much the same way, we might view caring as something of a double-
edged sword. As effective mentors, it is important that we care about the
people we are helping and are motivated by the prospect of them making
whatever transformation they are striving for: growing, developing, fulfilling some hidden potential or achieving their goals. However, part of our
usefulness to the learner is our objectivity, our distance from the issues and
concerns, our ability not only to provide a different perspective, but also to
leave responsibility with them. Caring too much can undermine this, turning empathy into sympathy and objectivity into partiality. The mentor suddenly, like "Fast Eddie," has a "stake" in the outcome, albeit an emotional
one rather than a financial one. Moreover, assuming a level of "caring" that

the quality of the relationship does not yet justify will inevitably appear false and inauthentic.

It is also worth noting the important role which humour plays in relationship-building. Not only are some of Sean's personal disclosures funny, but when Will finally starts to respond more constructively to Sean, in meeting four, it starts with him telling a joke about being on a plane. It is a good illustration of how humour can help to create a "safe space" in which difficult issues can be addressed. So, whilst enjoying the joke, Sean correctly reflects that Will has never been on a plane, gently challenging him again over his lack of real-life experience.

Given the Herculean struggle Sean has to engage in to earn his permission to work with Will, we might well ask ourselves why Will seems to open up so readily to Skyler, (other than the obvious reason that she is young, female and rather comely). After all, she is posh, privately-educated (Skyler? Really?) and attending Harvard, whose other students (admittedly male) Will seems to have nothing but contempt for. Once again, a sense of humour seems to help, but Sean is pretty much Skyler's equal in the kooky sense of humour stakes. It seems as though what Will responds to in Skyler is her utter lack of pretension, the fact that she is not putting on an act, not a phoney in Will's eyes. In other words, she is authentic. Also, she doesn't judge him. This too she has in common with Sean who, although sometimes highly judgemental of Will's arrogance and obnoxious behavior, still ultimately accepts him for what he is, as a person, not as a genius or as a psychiatric case.

CONCERN FOR THE INDIVIDUAL, NOT THE PROBLEM

This is perhaps the crux of their relationship. Gerry, Will's other "mentor," is concerned with Will's gifts and how he will use them, his potential contribution to the field of mathematics. Moreover, he cannot entirely put aside how puny Will's abilities make his own intellect seem. In other words, his concerns are for himself and for the problem at hand (how Will nurtures and deploys his talents). Maybe, like "Fast Eddie" Felson, Gerry too was tempted by the prospect of living vicariously through the younger prodigy and reinvigorating his own efforts in the field of mathematics by association with him. In marked contrast, Sean's concern is for Will the person. He wants to know about *him*, not what he knows. His interest is in Will's happiness and self-fulfilment, whatever form Will decides that should take. He sees it as Will's decision what he does, and vigorously defends Will against Gerry's efforts to steamroller him into a high-flying job, accusing the professor of manipulation. When Will tells him he's decided to go for the job interview, Sean first asks if this is what *Will* wants, *before* he congratulates him.

As with our vampires and hustlers, this is about the urge to help versus the urge to "fix." People may approach not only therapists like Sean, but also mentors, in the hope of receiving some resolution, some "cure." But many mentors, and indeed many psychotherapists, reject this perception of their role, as it denies the need for the learner/patient to be the architect of their own development and transition. As something of an aside, Sean's own attitude to life is also transformed by his work with Will, although, in contrast to "Fast Eddie," this is a welcome by-product of the process, not the intention he starts with.

SO, WHAT CAN WE LEARN....?

In summary, Sean's efforts to build a productive learning partnership with Will, against considerable odds, succeed for several reasons:

- He understands the need for permission to help, and a basic sense of trust before any rapport-building can bear fruit.
- He does not take it for granted that this will be there.
- He is patient in earning the right to help, and builds a "safe space" in which his learner can start to reveal his true self.
- He uses self-disclosure to build rapport and, in doing so, is not afraid to make himself vulnerable.
- He uses humour to build a sense of mutuality and equality.
- He is authentic and unpretentious, not phoney.
- Above all, his concern is entirely for the individual learner as a person, and not for himself or the learner's problem.

We can use these principles to construct a model which will help us reflect upon and develop our own attitude and approach to our mentoring practice. Trust is the oxygen of a successful learning dialogue. Without it, our best efforts to establish some rapport and honest, effective, two-way communication will be thwarted, regardless of what skills and techniques we deploy. Conversely, an abundance of mutual trust will turbo-charge our mentoring in a way no technique ever could. The operative term here is "mutual." The dangers of abusing the trust our learners place in us, whether deliberately or inadvertently, are manipulation and dependency. The learner ends up either pursuing a path not of their choosing, or achieving their goals at the expense of becoming dependent on their mentor, rather than enabled to make decisions and take action to fulfil their desires, as Will finally does when he goes off to be with the girl he loves.

Table 3.1.

	High Trust		Low Trust
Control	Control of both agenda and process with learner, promoting high sense of agency on their part. Power with learner	Control of agenda and process shared between learner and mentor. Some sense of agency on part of learner, but power shared, or mentor's power hidden	Control of agenda and process largely or wholly with mentor. Their power is abused and learner's sense of agency undermined
Orientation	Mentor's concern is primarily for the individual, largely motivated by learner achieving what they want	Concern is for both the individual and the problem/issue. Motivated by learner's agenda, provided it matches with what the mentor feels is appropriate/comfortable	Concern is largely for the problem/issue, or themselves. Mentor motivated by own gain and comfort only
Authenticity	Mentor is totally open about their feelings, values etc. Makes self vulnerable	Mentor discloses things about themselves, but is unable to be entirely open. Holds back	Mentor hides real feelings from learner, and even dissembles deliberately in order to get some result
Caring	Mentor genuinely cares about well-being of learner	Mentor struggles to care about learner's well-being, but maybe feigns concern	Mentor indifferent to well-being of learner. "It's just a job."
Humour	Both parties able to joke and tease without fear of causing offence. Sense of safe space	Limited sense of safety to see funny side of behavior or experiences. Inhibited by risk of offending	Little or no humour or fun in interchanges for fear of doing damage to relationship.
Impartiality	Mentor, whilst empathizing with learner, retains objectivity and neutrality to see alternatives and challenge	Learning partners so compatible that chemistry occasionally undermines mentor's ability to provide other options	Mentor either over-identifies with learner or is entirely driven by organizational needs which conflict with learner's goals/interests
Skills and techniques	Mentor uses communication skills and techniques transparently and helps learner to do same	Mentor uses appropriate range of communication skills in a reasonably transparent way	Mentor applies communications skills and techniques covertly to achieve what they see as right result

We have not dealt here with the mechanics of "contracting" in a mentoring partnership. It goes without saying that, as a way of ensuring some joint oversight of the use and abuse of trust in the relationship, all responsible mentors would regard this as a minimum safeguard. But in terms of a structure for reviewing and reflecting on our own coaching and mentoring partnerships specifically in the light of what the protagonists in these stories have taught us, we would offer the framework shown in Table 3.1. Most of us probably strive to keep to the left-hand side of this matrix most of the time, but perfection is not always achievable. Try assessing where you would place various learning partnerships of your own under each of our criteria.

REFERENCES

[1]Egan, G. (2002). *The Skilled Helper*, Pacific Grove, CA: Brooks/Cole.

[2]Scandura, T. (1998). Dysfunctional mentoring relationships and outcomes, *Journal of Management, 24*(3).

[3]Gravells, J. (2006). Mentoring Start-up entrepreneurs in the East Midlands – Troubleshooters and Trusted Friends, *The International Journal of Coaching and Mentoring, IV*(2), 20–21.

[4]Daloz, L. (1999). *Mentor,* San Francisco, CA: Jossey-Bass, 1999. (p. 246) and research by David Clutterbuck presented at Oxford Brookes University Coaching & Mentoring Conference 2007.

[5]Knight, A., & Poppleton, A. (2007). *Coaching in Organizations,* CIPD Research Insight report, Ashridge Centre for Coaching.

[6]Hardingham, A., Brearley, M., Moorhouse, A., & Venter, B. (2004). *The Coach's Coach,* London: CIPD.

[7]Herzberg, F. (1959). *The Motivation to Work,* New York: JohnWiley & Sons.

Films and Books

Jordan, N. (Director). (1994). *Interview with the Vampire* [Motion picture]. US: Geffen Pictures. (From the novel by Anne Rice (1976), published by Alfred A. Knopf, Inc., New York.)

Scorcese. M. (Director). (1986). *The Color of Money.* [Motion picture]. Burbank, CA: Touchstone Pictures. (From the novel by Walter Tevis (1984), published by Warner Books.)

van Sant, Gus. (Director). (1997). *Good Will Hunting* [Motion picture]. US: Lawrence Bender Productions.

CHAPTER 4

FROM THE BADA-BING TO THE BELLY OF THE WHALE (BY WAY OF BELGIUM)

The Mentor as Moral Compass and Conscience

THE SOPRANOS

We begin our meditation on the moral responsibilities of the mentor by returning briefly to *The Sopranos*, which, you will recall, is the saga of a fictional New Jersey gangster struggling like the rest of us to meet the often conflicting demands of family and career. Towards the end of the series, in the sixth and final season, Tony Soprano's analyst, Jennifer Melfi, finally refuses to continue their therapeutic relationship. The interventions of her own supervisor, other colleagues and her estranged husband, which she has resisted for five seasons, eventually convince her. The realization dawns that she is not only wasting her time but almost certainly doing harm. She realizes that Tony, far from responding to their sessions by modifying his anti-social behavior is actually using therapy to justify his actions and decisions, adopting strategies suggested by their discussions to become a more effective mob boss.

For example, Melfi raises the possibility of Tony easing his fraught relationship with Livia, his mother, by letting her feel she is getting her own way occasionally. What does Tony do but go away and use the same strategy to take control of his crime family by suggesting his elderly Uncle Junior become boss, despite Tony secretly pulling the strings in the background. We are even shown a book Tony is reading, called *Eldercare: Coping with Late-Life Crisis*. On numerous occasions we get the sense that Tony is using therapy to reconcile his violent crimes with his need for the self-image of someone who is not all bad, a loving father and a local business man. He invents justifications, based on his own twisted moral code, portraying himself as a "soldier," for example, who is entitled to kill other "soldiers," and differentiating himself from the "twisted and demented psychos" who deserve to go to hell.[1] These are self-deceptions, clearly, but ones which Dr. Melfi finds herself facilitating.

In this chapter we will examine this moral dimension to the mentor's role. What exactly do we see as our obligation to our learners, and how do we square this with our responsibility towards others and to our own system of values and beliefs? We may not find ourselves engaging with master criminals and murderous gangsters, but we will undoubtedly encounter learners whose values and moral code are perhaps different from our own.

> MENTOR: It was probably around my fourth or fifth meeting with Anil that it dawned on me all was not well. We had identified that relationships with his team and peer group were topics he particularly wanted to work on. He had always been a task-focused individual, and his discomfort with the whole idea of relationship-building as part of the work environment was not just down to a lack of interpersonal skills, but probably stemmed from a personality and value set that genuinely failed to see why "getting on with people" was important, so long as you did your job well. Whilst finding his attitude to others rather hard to warm to, I obviously avoided appearing in any way judgemental. I had been pleased with how enthusiastically Anil had responded to our exploration of listening, "matching" and other rapport-building strategies, and ways in which he could identify influencing role-models within the organization and experiment with these behaviors. I tried to couch our discussions in terms of the rich variety of behaviors leaders may draw upon, rather than try to identify any one recipe as the "correct" one. It was only when he recounted a story of how he had used elements of these influencing skills to persuade an older

member of his team to volunteer for redundancy that I began to question what, if anything, I had done wrong....

MENTOR: Valerie was a senior surgical consultant at the hospital, whom I had been working with for several months. Most of our conversations had revolved around her difficulties with establishing a reasonable work-life balance, and coping with a job that, at times, entailed very high levels of stress. When she turned up for our fourth or fifth session in a state of what appeared quite clearly to me to be considerable intoxication, I had no way of empirically testing her fitness for work, and was conscious of how prone to alcoholism people in her situation were. But I was also acutely conscious of the potential for her harming others in such a condition, and, despite myself, felt outraged at her irresponsibility. I saw it as my duty to terminate the conversation immediately and report her to hospital management....

MENTOR: Benjamin was under pressure to make savings, and had decided that he needed to "sort out" a new member of staff, Wendy, who had been struggling in the job. My own observation was that Benjamin's reasoning seemed to have a lot to do with Wendy being female, recently married and openly talking about trying to start a family. I felt comfortable challenging him about this, as his mentor, albeit to no avail, as it was clearly at odds with both the law and stated organizational policies. But I felt more ambivalent about pushing him hard on doing more to help Wendy lift her performance before going for the easy option of dismissal. I was conscious that this was a reflection of my particular moral stance, rather than a reflection of how Benjamin, or for that matter his organization, really saw the world, and it was they who were paying my bill. Maybe I should just have ended the mentoring relationship, but that seemed a bit of a cop-out too.....

ENABLING, BUT NOT IN A GOOD WAY...

Sitting back in his office in the "Bada-Bing," the New Jersey strip joint and lap-dancing club that acts as his HQ, Tony Soprano remains a violent and brutal mobster in spite of four years of "learning conversations" with his well-intentioned therapist. The only difference that his relationship with Dr. Melfi has made is that now he is a violent and brutal mobster who has discovered a process for justifying his behavior and more effectively manipulating the behavior of others to his own immoral ends. Not only has Melfi's work with Tony failed to result in any substantial change, but his criminal activity and cynical exploitation of others may in some way have been strengthened.

If Dr. Melfi's colleagues are correct, his sessions with her have really only been the opportunity for a self-indulgent dialogue; a dialogue which he has learned to exploit in order to analyze and justify his behavior in an environment which is far more non-judgemental and morally accommodating than the outside world would be. The implication is that, in creating this environment in which to explore his experiences and emotions, Dr. Melfi has unintentionally become complicit in Tony Soprano's morally distorted way of life, and acted as an enabler to his dysfunctional activities and goals. It is true that Melfi is a psychotherapist and not a mentor, but the idea that any one-to-one helping relationship, by focusing so resolutely on the individual and their needs, might unwittingly become perversely enabling in such a way is just as relevant to mentors and their role. Like the characters in this drama, are we too not at risk of becoming victims of our growing self-help culture? In a modern (and predominantly western) world, where finding one's potential, achieving self-actualization and reaching one's personal goals, however ambitious, are seen almost as a basic human right, what place have "old-fashioned" values such as duty, selflessness and service to others? At one point, in a satirical sideswipe at this social trend, Jennifer Melfi questions how many people will have to die for Tony's "personal growth."

As mentors, we too are focused primarily on the needs of our learners, and for the large part rightly so. But maybe ours is also an activity which too easily promotes the pre-eminence of personal growth at the expense of other, equally important considerations. Is there a danger that, like Jennifer Melfi, mentors may unwittingly become a kind of dysfunctional enabler? In other words, we work so hard not to be judgemental or directive with our learners that we end up reinforcing values and becoming complicit in behaviors, of which we or society at large would disapprove. By avoiding conflict, whether in the interests of rapport or neutrality or even a need to be liked, might we sometimes be guilty of allowing questionable assumptions, values and moral choices to go unchallenged? If we even partially accept that such dangers are lurking in the shadows, waiting for unwary mentors, then surely it obliges us at least to have a very strong sense of our own moral code, if only in order to know when to refuse or abandon a learning relationship which is proving toxic. OK, it may be questionable to extrapolate such an argument from a fictional therapist in a gangster drama, who is not even a mentor anyway; but there already exists a relatively small, but compelling body of evidence on the dangers of mentoring and coaching.[2] And whilst most of this, as we have discussed already, focuses on the learner being manipulated by the mentor, there is evidence that it can cut both ways. This "dark side" to mentoring, like Dr. Melfi's experience, suggests that mentors must at least be alert to the possibility of unwitting complicity with values and behaviors that they might find unacceptable.

MORALITY AND ETHICS ON THE AGENDA

At the time of writing, the emphasis on morality in the leadership and management literature continues to grow. The scandals of Enron and World Com and others gave way to the global "credit crunch" and the sense that banks and other financial institutions had made huge short-term profits at the expense of long-term fiscal viability. The story was that banking bosses on both sides of the Atlantic, earned themselves big, fat bonuses whilst unleashing massive hardship and suffering on millions of ordinary people. In the U.K. this coincided with a growing row over members of Parliament claiming expenses to which they were either legally, or at best morally, not entitled. Unsurprisingly, the need for leaders to behave more ethically and to pack a "moral compass" somewhere in that kitbag of skills, attributes and techniques has become widely recognized. Students graduating from Harvard's MBA programme have been inspired to take an oath to "serve the common good."[3] All these big, global organizations are now awash with social responsibility policies, ethical standards and risk management departments. These do not, on the face of it, seem to have stemmed the tide of selfish and greedy behavior. Commentators note that decisions are still ultimately taken by individuals, and individuals choose whether or not to abide by the policies and standards. It is worth pointing out that many of these individuals, these senior executives, particularly in the financial services sector, will have probably employed executive coaches and mentors, maybe even to talk through some of the dilemmas and decisions they were facing.

Yet a cornerstone of most mentoring models is the need to be non-judgemental. Many mentors will attest to the importance of "unconditional positive regard" in their orientation towards the learner. This originally psychotherapeutic concept, as defined by Carl Rogers,[4] refers to the way a therapist provides total acceptance of their client, regardless of what they may say or do, in order to help them accept and take responsibility for themselves. In many forums outside of psychotherapy this concept also goes pretty much unchallenged, and yet how sure are we of its uncritical application to mentoring? Does it mean that we must positively accept the learner regardless of the extent to which their attitudes and behavior might be repellent to us or even to wider society? After all, there are times when the mentor quite rightly plays the role of arch-questioner of the status quo, emphasizing enquiry, learning and multiple interpretations of reality. Mentors and, for that matter, coaches will even act as "conscience" to the learner, maybe helping them to police and challenge behaviors they wish to change.[5] So how do we reconcile these legitimate needs for acceptance, support and challenge whilst remaining true to our own notions of right and wrong? Is it even our place to play the role of moral compass and conscience?

DEXTER

Those readers already aghast that the term "police" has crept into a discussion of the mentor's role, should maybe stop reading now, before we start introducing "serial killer" and "vigilante" into the discourse. For the television series *Dexter*, produced by Showtime, and based on the books by Jeff Lindsay, concerns a Miami forensics expert, Dexter Morgan, played by Michael C. Hall, who, after traumatically witnessing his mother's brutal and bloody death as a young child, has been left a supposedly "incurable," sociopathic serial-killer. Organized, efficient, deadly, and unable to forge genuine human relationships, he successfully fakes chummy bonhomie with colleagues, his step-sister and even a girl-friend, whilst stalking the Floridian resort despatching evil-doers with an array of butcher's knives, after strapping them naked to a table with cling-film. His mentor is (or was) Harry, the policeman who discovered him at his mother's murder scene and became his foster father. In flashback we learn that, as Dexter gets older and his peculiar condition becomes apparent to his foster father, Harry decides that his son's bloodlust cannot be cured, so the only option is to enable him to use it for "good." For Harry, using it for good means killing only the vilest criminals who have escaped justice, and he sets about mentoring Dexter, schooling him in forensic detection and his own moral code, in order to ensure that Dexter only kills bad guys and never gets caught doing it.

There are of course a number of problems with this, and it should be acknowledged that this tongue-in-cheek drama is pretty self-aware about all of them. For a start, helping your sociopathic foster son become a vigilante serial-killer is not really the only option. Having him locked up in a secure institution, whilst leaving you open to accusations of political incorrectness, is probably still the alternative most of us would choose. More importantly, though, enabling your learner to summarily execute people, however heinous their crimes, by subjecting them to abduction, torture and death, followed by dismemberment and an anonymous watery grave, is not really what you would call helping them use their strengths for good.

IMPOSING ONE'S OWN MORAL CODE

Not only would most of us take issue with Harry's idea of what is "good," but, even if we went along with the whole, vigilante, "ridding the streets of scum," approach to justice, we might still have severe reservations about the million and one things that could go wrong with such demented social engineering, (as later episodes of the drama begin to reveal). Here we have a mentor, who is not only deciding the agenda for his learner's development, but imposing his own version of a moral framework upon the whole learning relationship. Harry is an extreme, but nevertheless, potent illustration of why mentors must avoid imposing their own values on their learners. As soon as we do this, we not only imply that our code is the correct one and we are sole arbiters of right and wrong, but we also become more directly responsible for the learner's consequent actions.

So, if we fail to challenge enough, or to abandon learners to whom we are unable to show unconditional positive regard, we can, like Jennifer Melfi, become complicit in behavior which we may find immoral. But, on the other hand, if we impose our own personal values and standards on our learners, like Harry, we may find ourselves taking even more responsibility for any subsequent behavioral difficulties that result. In an attempt to work our way out of this ethical cleft stick, let us turn to by far the most dark and horrific of our stories so far.

PINOCCHIO

Jiminy Cricket is companion to the eponymous boy-puppet in Disney's 1940 cartoon feature *Pinocchio,* adapted from the traditional fairy tale by Carlo Collodi. Having stumbled upon Pinocchio and his creator after seeking shelter in Geppetto's workshop, Jiminy is appointed to the job of official conscience by the Blue Fairy, despite his initial scepticism about the power of fate and wishes coming true. He sees his role as guiding Pinocchio along the "straight and narrow path," and helping him to tell right from wrong.

As a mentor, Jiminy is nothing if not judgemental, and, on first appearances, he is not a hugely successful conscience either. He continually loses track of the puppet, leaving the way open for the unscrupulous "Honest John" and Gideon the cat to tempt Pinocchio away from school and into all sorts of misbehavior. When he sees Pinocchio performing in Stromboli's show he moodily assumes that he's no longer needed, and when he finally catches up with his charge, sitting caged in the back of the evil showman's gypsy caravan, it is only to join Pinocchio in wallowing in their bad fortune.

Yet, by the end of the story, Pinocchio has proved himself brave, truthful and unselfish, thus earning his reward of becoming a real boy, and Jiminy is being awarded an eighteen carat gold badge by the Blue Fairy for services to the honourable profession of personal conscience. Why?

A CRITICAL FRIEND INDEED

Well, to most of us, Jiminy certainly has a healthier sense of what is right and what is wrong than does Dexter's mentor and foster father, Harry. He sees right through the promises of easy fortune and selfish pleasure that so seduce the naïve young puppet-boy. Furthermore, as Jiminy himself points out, he is more of a genuine friend to Pinocchio than others, such as the feckless Lampwick, will ever be. This is because, however critical he might be of Pinocchio's behavior, he genuinely cares about Pinocchio's well-being and is both patient and committed to helping him succeed. In fact, his commitment goes as far as following his young protégé into the sea to rescue Geppetto from the belly of Monstro, the whale. (If wooden boys and sea water are an unhappy mix, then small insects and fish are surely even more so.) All in all, Jiminy proves to be an effective "critical friend," displaying a true belief in his learner's ability eventually to walk the "straight and narrow path," sticking with Pinocchio through thick and thin, and reminding him of his promise to the Blue Fairy, in spite of setbacks and rebuffs. In all these respects the dapper little insect does have something to teach us.

CONSCIENCE AND SELF-DETERMINATION

However, patience, commitment and support are not what distinguish Jiminy from Harry; and if Harry's sense of right and wrong is less palatable to us than the cricket's, well, surely that's a matter of opinion?

No, the really significant difference here is that Jiminy challenges and chides, but does not impose his moral code on Pinocchio in such a way as to directly influence his actions. He is *meant* to be small, and only intermittently and indirectly influential. He is the physical representation of that still, small voice in all of us that, with varying effectiveness, challenges the moral and ethical basis on which we are making decisions: in other words, our conscience. He is pretty hopeless at making Pinocchio behave according to his wishes. All he can do is be there to challenge the puppet's thinking at crucial moments. Pinocchio does not actually prove himself brave, truthful and unselfish in direct response to the instructions of his "conscience." This transformation finally occurs when he is confronted by a challenging event, his father's capture by Monstro, and he makes his *own* decision about what is the right course of action. So here we have a rather different take from both *The Sopranos* and *Dexter* on the idea of mentor as conscience.

Some thoughts so far:

- A good mentor sticks with the learner and continues to have faith in their ability to achieve their own transformation, in spite of incompatibilities and frustrations.
- Engaging with learners whose values and beliefs are incompatible with our own can be difficult from the perspective of building strong rapport, and maintaining "unconditional positive regard," but this

should not exclude us from exploiting the enormous learning potential inherent in mentoring those very different from ourselves, (and you don't get much more different than an insect in a suit and a sentient, independently mobile, wooden boy).

- A learner may require large doses of non-judgemental support from their mentor, in order to help them overcome fears, insecurities, or crises of self-confidence and self-esteem.
- If the mentor is to really make people think, and reflect upon their existing assumptions, values and beliefs, then they will at times have to challenge these.
- There is nothing wrong with a mentor bringing their own moral code to the learning relationship, nor in sharing it, just so long as they avoid imposing their own values and beliefs and moral code on their mentee.
- Successful change can only be achieved by the individual's own determination and so mentees must be allowed to make their own choices and decisions, regardless of whether these conform to the mentor's notions of what is right or wrong.
- The mentor can usefully challenge assumptions, decisions and behaviors. However, to claim either the credit or the responsibility for any direct cause and effect link between their dialogue with a mentee and the mentee's subsequent decisions and actions is to deny the learner's accountability for their own development. Jiminy Cricket can help Pinocchio become a real boy, but becoming a real boy has to be the puppet's own agenda. Jiminy gets a badge, in reward for his steadfast support, but it is Pinocchio who is author of his own transformation.

In case you are thinking at this point that such a rosy view of humankind's potential for redemption, with the help of mentor as conscience, is exactly what you might expect from Walt Disney, let us turn to another, more morally ambiguous narrative, albeit in a fairy-tale setting.

IN BRUGES

Written and directed by Martin McDonagh, *In Bruges* is a mix of violent gangster thriller, pitch-black comedy and eerily beautiful travelogue. It concerns a novice hit man, Ray (played by Colin Farrell) and his more experienced "mentor" Ken (Brendan Gleeson), who find themselves stranded in Bruges, hiding out after Ray's first "hit" has gone tragically wrong. In the opening voice-over Ray describes cleaning the blood off his hands in a Burger King and receiving instructions to get the f*** out of London and go to f****** Bruges. Clearly this is not Pinocchio; and Ken, himself an experienced assassin, and therefore hardly the voice of moral rectitude, is no Jiminy Cricket. Yet there is an equally instructive and entertaining dynamic in the relationship between these two very different men. Ken is older, calmer, even-tempered and polite. He enjoys the opportunity to sightsee around the cobbled medieval streets of Bruges and learn of its history. Ray, on the other hand, is young, brash, immature, volatile, aggressive and something of a bigot. Moody and restless, like a kid being dragged around on holiday, Ray steadfastly hates Bruges and anything related to its history and culture. As far as this mentoring relationship is concerned, not only is Ken quite clearly the senior partner, but, as in *Dexter,* it has a definite father-son quality to it.

Only part-way through the film do we learn the nature of Ray's dreadful crime. In fulfilling his first job, murdering a priest, he accidentally shoots dead a little boy knelt praying in the church. Ray is haunted by this act, and tortured by remorse for what he has done. For this is another world, like Tony Soprano's and Dexter Morgan's, in which relativism rules and concepts of morality, honour and integrity are bent and stretched to breaking point. Killing people who "deserve" it is not necessarily a cause for regret, but killing a child is beyond the pale. Whatever the priest may have done to "deserve" summary execution (the later implication is that he was guilty of child abuse), we might take the view that shooting anyone in cold blood is morally a bit dodgy, but the story invites us to enter a universe where the moral code is very different from our own. Ken is a hugely likeable and ultimately heroic character, despite murdering people for a living. Ray and Ken's boss, a wonderfully highly-strung East End gangster, played by Ralph Fiennes and also called Harry, abides by a strict, if distorted, code of honour, which makes child-murder punishable by death, and unflinchingly applies these "principles" to himself when he mistakes Jimmy, the dwarf actor, for a child, at the end of the film, after blowing most of his head off with a dum-dum bullet.

ACCEPTING THE LEARNER IN THEIR OWN CONTEXT....

The interesting thing is that we find ourselves relating to these characters in the context of their own moral code, however repugnant that might be to us. Ken, the mentor here, perseveres in supporting his young colleague, even sacrificing his life, steadfast in his belief that Ray has a shot at redemption and deserves to be allowed to take it. The fact that the story takes place at Christmas not only adds to the general, fairy-tale beauty of the setting, but also reinforces the religious undertones. Trapped in his personal purgatory of Bruges, reflected in the religious imagery surrounding them, and in particular the Hieronymus Bosch painting he and Ken see in the art gallery, Ray desperately asks his partner if he believes in sin, guilt, hell and judgement. Ken's answer is no, he believes in "trying to live a good life," (despite the inconvenience of his career). His world view, tainted by his own ambiguous feelings about his crimes and a pragmatic blurring of moral certainties, contrasts sharply with Ray's agonisingly black and white take on things. In this regard Ken is not the confident arbiter of right and wrong that Jiminy Cricket is, and yet, just like him, he ends up putting his own life in danger in order to help someone else transform themselves and live a "better" life. When Ken goes to the park to kill Ray, on Harry's orders, and finds him about to commit suicide, he not only fails to shoot him, but prevents him from shooting himself, (something Harry is later understandably incredulous about). It is an intentionally comic scene, but also possibly the point at which Ken becomes finally convinced of Ray's capacity for redemption. At this point he resolves to give Ray the chance of salvation and take full responsibility with an incandescent Harry.

... AND BELIEVING IN THEIR CAPACITY TO CHANGE

Whilst we can argue that this is not difficult for Ken, a man who is in no position to judge Ray, or be morally offended by his actions, nevertheless we should not underestimate how difficult a man to love Ray really is. After all, he hates culture and learning, is prejudiced and abusive to dwarves, overweight people, and other nationalities (notably Americans), takes drugs, steals from his date, punches a man and his girlfriend who annoy him in a restaurant, oh, and yes, he murders people for a living. Yet, it is a measure of the cleverness of both script and acting, as well as our own capacity to accept people in the context of their own particular world, that we find ourselves rooting for Ray, and even, at times empathizing with his responses. More surprising than the fact that Ken can find it in his heart to support and help Ray at the cost of his own life, is the fact that *we* are also able to suspend our judgment of his heinous crimes in order to see what Ken calls his "capacity to change" and to "do something with his life." At the end of the story, we are left not knowing whether Ray, having been shot several times by Harry in a pretty terminal-looking way, will survive and make it out of Bruges to whatever his personal vision of heaven might be. In a way this does not matter. It is the fact that, despite everything, we want him to survive that is at the same time both significant and slightly unsettling.

As in *Pinocchio*, this story of murder and mayhem in Belgium presents us with the view that an individual has the capacity for change and improvement, whatever their past misdeeds and however apparently dysfunctional their current grasp of right and wrong. Both mentors stick with their learners and endure significant personal sacrifice (one is swallowed by a whale, the other gets a bullet in the neck and then leaps over a hundred feet onto cobbles) in support of their conviction that their learner is capable of transformation.

"UNCONDITIONAL POSITIVE REGARD"

This brings us back to Carl Rogers and the application of "unconditional positive regard." Wilkins, in an article re-assessing the concept, cites a client who was a misogynist and a racist, but argues that accepting him was about acknowledging his worldview as a product of his experience, rather than about approving or disapproving of his values as such.[6,7] Furthermore, goes the argument, a person can only change if they truly accept who they are, and in this they can be helped significantly by the therapist (or mentor) accepting them for who they are. The implication of this argument for mentors is clear. In order to be effective, we must accept the learner for who they are, as a product of their particular upbringing and experience, without judging. After all, we can find ourselves "rooting for" Ray, without agreeing with his peculiar set of values. But can practising mentors in the real world always hope to emulate Ken and Jiminy's unfailing commitment to continue supporting an individual, no matter how far from the mentor's idea of a straight and narrow path they stray? We acknowledge in the contracting process that both parties may have boundaries, and many mentors will highlight their ethical obligation to take some action if, for example, they perceive a risk of the learner harming themselves or others. How often do we stop and consider what harming others really means, and how widely we see this obligation applying?

IT'S NOT JUST ABOUT YOU TWO

Following the logic above, let us suppose you are mentoring someone who expresses overtly racist views, and let us further suppose that these are directly opposed to your own values. As a good mentor, you may seek first to explore and fully understand these views and the assumptions and experiences on which they are based. Having first sought to understand and accept the learner for who they are without judging, you might then feel it legitimate to intervene and challenge these assumptions and views. Once the learner has been challenged and introduced to an alternative perspective, you rightly leave the learner to draw their own conclusion, make their own decision, and plan their own action accordingly. But then what? What if this person's decision is to stick to their beliefs and spend their time promoting ideas and policies which increase inter-racial hatred and tension? What if the individual concerned is heading up an organization with a multi-ethnic workforce? Or, to take an entirely different, but particularly topical illustration, what if you were mentoring a senior banking executive who you knew was taking more than the usual levels of risk in their borrowing, and was facilitating the extension of loans to individuals barely able to repay them? What is your obligation to others outside the mentoring relationship and what would your definition of doing harm be?

"GIVE A LITTLE WHISTLE!"

At this point we must surely address what role the mentor's own sense of right and wrong plays. We have noted already the dangers of imposing our values onto the learner, but what else can we learn from Jiminy and Ken, or the stories of Jennifer Melfi and Harry Morgan, whose no doubt well-meaning interventions become so morally untenable?

Our standard ethical safeguard against doing harm, or enabling others to do harm is to leave conclusions, decisions and actions in the hands of the learner, and avoid exercising control over their lives which might lead to manipulation and dependency (see Chapter 2). But either we "help" or we don't. Surely if mentoring is worth doing at all, it must be enabling in some way. In this respect we are like any other consultant or advisor. We cannot accept the satisfaction of "helping" people to learn, change and achieve their goals, without also accepting some responsibility for the outcome. Yes, we can say that we are only, like Ken, facilitating change. We are just giving people the reflective space in which to examine their experience and make their own decisions, for which they must take all responsibility, but is this not just a convenient simplification? Ken "saves" Ray; his intervention actively preventing his execution and offering him the chance to go on and fulfil whatever potential he may have in him. In a similar way Jiminy Cricket saves Pinocchio from Pleasure Island and a lifetime spent as a donkey, working in the salt mines. We know Pinocchio takes the chance he has been given and uses it to do the "right thing" and rescue Gepetto. But we never find out if Ray survives Bruges to change his ways. If Ray survives only to mess up another murder and kill another innocent child, rather than found an orphanage in Romania and find a cure for the common cold, would Ken not feel a bit responsible? (If he were not being scraped up from Bruges Market Square with a putty knife, that is.) What if your learner's values, morality and resulting behavior towards others remain steadfastly at odds with your own?

WHERE DO YOU DRAW THE LINE?

Our view would be that you consider another, perhaps more controversial principle:

- Mentors should be very aware of and clear about what their own value set and moral code are, and avoid becoming complicit or appearing to be complicit in supporting activities which contravene these standards.

The problem is that, without this principle, mentors leave themselves vulnerable to a charge of convenient moral and ethical elasticity. In other words, however much we claim to be a "blank canvas," a non-judgemental mirror reflecting back our learners' ideas and experiences and decisions in order to help them become whatever they want to become, we cannot really escape our responsibility so easily for helping them to do whatever they end up doing.

Ask yourself this question. Are there any circumstances under which you would definitely withdraw from a mentoring relationship on moral grounds (and we are distinguishing between this and other reasons one might agree to terminate a mentoring relationship, such as chemistry, fit or timing)? This is where considering extreme cases like Tony Soprano, Dexter or Ray the apprentice hitman, may come in useful. If the answer is yes, as I suspect it would be with most mentors, then we must accept the principle that there are people out there towards whom we are unable or unwilling to offer open-ended, unconditional, positive regard. If this is the case, it then becomes a matter for the individual mentor to determine where, for them, the dividing line is drawn. If, for you, this is simply a matter of staying the right side of the law, then you might be tempted to fall back on this simple formula. But, does this include all laws or is it only relevant to make such decisions when the illegal activity is something connected to the mentoring itself? Once we start making distinctions between different laws and the extent to which our mentoring is relevant to any moral or ethical conflict, we may find ourselves in largely uncharted waters unless we have thought carefully about what we believe, and what values and moral code we will adhere to in managing our mentoring relationships. Hence our suggestion that knowing where you stand as an individual is vital to helping the mentor make decisions about what they are prepared to accept unconditionally, what and when they will challenge, and at what point they are uncomfortable with supporting and enabling a particular individual.

SUMMARY

So, what have these stories to tell us about how mentors should go about identifying and observing any moral responsibility they may have towards their learners and society at large? There are a number of conclusions we might draw from what we have discussed:

- Mentors have a responsibility to focus primarily on their learner's agenda and needs, to help them achieve their aims, and to do them no harm. But they cannot escape a responsibility to society at large to avoid enabling behavior that may harm others.
- Mentors should not judge their learners, but neither should they allow themselves to become complicit in supporting activities which contravene society's accepted codes of behavior.
- Considerable self-awareness and vigilance is required of mentors in walking the line between supportive, positive regard and collusion and complicity. This is partly an issue for contracting, but also demands attention in reflective practice and supervision.
- Mentors should not take the place of the learner's own conscience, nor impose their own values and moral code on the learner.
- However, mentors do have a legitimate role to play as supplementary "conscience" and as challenger of values and moral standards, provided that this is agreed with the learner, and provided these roles are accompanied by a genuine belief in the learner's capacity to achieve whatever transformation in knowledge, behavior, skills or beliefs they themselves have identified.
- We should not shy away from mentoring those whose value system is very different from our own because this can present unrivalled potential for mutual learning. But our conviction of people's capacity to change, and our ability to accept them in the context of their particular circumstances and moral universe will not prevent us from occasionally finding ourselves unable to continue supporting someone.
- Knowing our own values and moral boundaries allows us to make choices about whom we are prepared to accept unconditionally, what and when we will challenge, and at what point we are uncomfortable with supporting and enabling a particular individual.
- We might choose to stick with a particular learner whose values and behavior conflict with what we subscribe to, so long as this harms no-one else and we feel able to continue challenging these values productively. Alternatively, we may reluctantly decide to terminate a relationship which we feel is becoming dysfunctionally enabling. Such decisions are partly a matter for our own conscience.
- But what we should avoid is sticking with a mentoring relationship where we have become complicit in behavior which undermines either our own moral code or that of society at large, where harm to others may result, or where we are unable to continue challenging without losing mutual trust and respect.

REFERENCES

[1]Greene, R., & Vernezze, P. (Eds.). (2004). *The Sopranos and Philosophy,* Chicago: Open Court.

[2]Examples include: Berglas, S. (2002). The Very Real dangers of Executive Coaching" *Harvard Business Review, 80*(6); Eby, L., Butts, M., Lockwood, A., & Shana, S. (2004). Protégés' negative mentoring experiences, *Personnel Psychology, 57*(2).

[3]Foreswearing Greed. *The Economist,* June 6th 2009.

[4]Rogers, C. (1951). *Client-centred therapy,* Boston: Houghton Mifflin.

[5]Hardingham, A., Brearley, M., Moorhouse, A., & Venter, B. (2004). *The Coach's Coach,* London: CIPD.

[6]Wilkins, P. (2000). Unconditional positive regard reconsidered, *British Journal of Guidance & Counselling, 28*(1), 23–36.

[7]Stokes, P. (2003). Exploring the relationship between mentoring and counselling, *British Journal of Guidance & Counselling, 31*(1).

Television, Films and Books

Chase, D. (Producer). (1986). *The Sopranos* [Television series]. New York: HBO. (Ran from 1999 to 2007.)

Disney, W. (Producer). (1940). *Pinocchio* [Motion picture]. Burbank, CA: Disney. (Adapted from the original fairy tale, *Pinocchio – Tale of a Puppet* by Carlo Collodi [1883].)

Manos, Jr., J. (Creator). (2006–present). *Dexter* [Television series]. New York: Showtime. (From the novels by Jeff Lindsay.)

McDonagh, M. (Writer/Director). (2008). *In Bruges* [Motion picture]. London: Film 4.

CHAPTER 5

RATSO, RITA AND THE ANDROID

Personal Change and Self-Fulfilment

JOURNEY TO SELF-FULFILMENT

In the previous chapter we explored Jiminy Cricket's key role as mentor in the tale of *Pinocchio*. We're going to begin this chapter by looking again at Pinocchio himself and his journey from puppet to boy. Fashioned from wood by his "father" Gepetto, this puppet without strings isn't content to remain a mere facsimile. His name means literally "eye of pine" or "wooden eye." If we think of the eyes as a window to the soul, we have here a creature who walks and talks but can neither perceive the world clearly nor relate authentically, "eye to eye," with others. His goal is to become human, and to do this he needs to change and to develop qualities he doesn't at first possess. The tale itself is an account of his adventures in pursuit of this personal goal of self-fulfilment; and, as such, it presents us with a metaphor signifying every individual's journey towards developing their full potential, to see the world clearly and without delusion, and to relate honestly to themselves and others. We might call this a quest to become one's "best self" – a goal which Abraham Maslow[1] has called "self-actualization."

But, as Pinocchio's journey illustrates, personal change and self-fulfilment are not always easily achieved, and may sometimes involve not only a cost to ourselves but to others, too. Such collateral damage in Pinocchio's case involved his "father" being held captive; while for the busy non-puppet professional the single-minded pursuit of such goals might mean, for example, a parent, partner or child being neglected or marginalized. In this chapter we shall be looking at the possible consequences of undertaking a process of personal change, and at the different guises that mentoring may take if the learner is to be accompanied and supported on their journey towards self-understanding. We shall be exploring what is meant by the idea of becoming more authentic or "more human," and questioning the place of theories of this kind in an unequal society. We shall be asking whether it is necessary for the mentor themselves to have achieved some degree of personal change and self-fulfilment before they can provide effective support to the learner.

But first let's see briefly how Pinocchio's journey can be used to illustrate some important features of the process of so-called "self-actualization" which this chapter will go on to explore and evaluate.

- **Agency and free will:** Pinocchio doesn't simply resign himself to being a puppet for the rest of his life. He doesn't make the assumption that because he's started life as a wooden toy, that's all he's ever going to be able to be. He becomes actively involved in shaping his own fate, demonstrating a belief in free will rather than assuming that his life's trajectory is pre-determined by what has gone before.
- **Setting goals:** The puppet sets himself a goal: to become a human boy. Despite the emphasis in the film's theme song – *When you wish upon a star* – upon dreaming and wish fulfilment, Pinocchio's goal is not, in the context of a fairy tale, impossible. And it is a positive one which, after some false starts, he is willing to work hard towards.
- **Seeking personal change:** Pinocchio's goal is about personal change (quite literally in his case) and self-fulfilment. We see that, in order to achieve his goal, he must undergo a process of change. In the journey towards self actualization we have to let go of our old selves. Superficial changes in appearance or behavior won't be enough to get us there. In fact there are two particularly important aspects of change which Pinocchio exemplifies. One is about *gaining in virtue* – what we might call "becoming good," or personal improvement. The other is about becoming more "real" or more *authentic* – more truly himself.
- **Willingness to learn:** After falling for Honest John Fox's bogus quick fix approach, Pinocchio eventually realizes that learning is an inevitable part of the process of personal change. He never does get to

school, but he certainly begins to learn some lessons. Two of the most important ones are that personal change cannot be accomplished without hard work; and that although on the way to changing for the better there will inevitably be the occasional relapse, it is important to persevere.

PUPPETS AND ANDROIDS: BECOMING MORE HUMAN

There's an additional layer of meaning that we can take from the story of Pinocchio, and that's the idea of what it means to become "human." We sometimes talk about someone becoming "more human." We can take this literally if we're talking about a wooden puppet: he wants to become flesh and blood – something he originally very patently was not. But what about if we were to apply the same phrase to a work colleague or line manager? Our meaning then becomes less transparent and more difficult to define because we will be speaking figuratively. We might say, for example:

> I'd get on better with Gill at work if she tried to be a bit more human. And I think she'd be happier, too. In fact it would be better for everyone's motivation, all round.

Clearly we're not talking here about Gill running without batteries or getting up off all fours and unclenching her teeth from the postal worker's trousers. We're talking rather about wanting her to exhibit a set of qualities which we associate with being an enlightened, evolved, fully socialized human being. These qualities may include, for example, the willingness to be sympathetic, approachable and reasonable, and the ability to face up to her own faults and vulnerabilities, and to admit to her mistakes. Or it may be – on an altogether more superficial level – simply about not invading colleagues' space, and remembering to ask after their families once in a while. Either way, what we seem to mean here by "being human" includes behavior which denotes a level of self-awareness and an awareness of the feelings of others – both key aspects of emotional intelligence.

The process of "becoming more human" is illustrated in an interesting way in the cult TV series *Star Trek: The Next Generation,* in which a continuing story line concerns the efforts of the android, Data, who holds the rank of Commander on the star ship *Enterprise,* to understand what it means to be human, and to acquire the qualities which will make him appear more so. His mentor in this project is his captain, Jean-Luc Picard, played by the excellent Shakespearean actor, Patrick Stewart. From episode to episode and series to series Picard patiently answers Data's questions about the nature and purpose of emotion and feelings, while himself providing a role model of the noblest behavior and highest virtues to which a human might aspire. Data is on an *ontological* quest (*ontology* being the study of the nature of being) which is all the more urgent and poignant for his being a "mere" machine. But it is a quest on which all of us could be – and many of us are – engaged to some degree or another. Data's goals are clear; and over the several series he does begin to gain more understanding of what it means to be human. One of the ways he does this is through an engagement with music and literature, art forms which are capable of conveying the full range of human emotions. And we know that it's not only fictional androids who can benefit from "learning" about emotion in this way. As we saw in Chapter One (where we refer to Rorty's claims about fiction), literature can provide us with a vicarious experience of others' circumstances, others' joys and worries. Such experience, albeit at second-hand, helps us to see beyond ourselves, to feel how it might be to stand in another's shoes, and to acquire the sensibility towards others which is an essential part of personal growth and development.

Gradually Data begins to exhibit qualities of loyalty and attachment. And together with this he seems to develop a moral sense – an understanding of what is right and wrong, as opposed to simply what is logical or expedient. Indeed, this ability to know what is good and what is evil becomes central to Data's goal of personal growth and integration. Here he is heavily reliant at first on the integrity and sure moral compass of his mentor. But, unlike Pinocchio and Tony Soprano, Data is from the beginning keen *to learn* and is willing to trust absolutely and to follow enthusiastically the ethical guidance and example which his mentor provides. Data remains an android, but he does succeed by the final series in developing a degree of sensitivity, self-knowledge and moral judgement which are undoubtedly qualities which any true human would aspire to. He and his Captain, therefore, can be seen as an example of the way the goals of personal change and self-fulfilment can be positively pursued with the support and encouragement of skilful mentoring. And although Data, unlike Pinocchio, never does quite succeed in his goal of becoming human, this does not invalidate his quest. Perhaps it would be more accurate to say that Data had a "dream" of becoming human, which he knew all along was not realistic, but which propelled him nevertheless to become the best he could be. This distinction between dreams and goals is something we shall return to later in the chapter.

We might say that Data and Pinocchio both sought to become more "real." But what do we mean when we apply this to ourselves, we who are already human? Going back to the unfortunate Gill, mentioned earlier, we saw her colleague expressing the wish that she would be "more human." Is this the same thing as being "more real"? Probably not. When we talk about "self-fulfilment" or about becoming our "authentic self" we are referring to a whole group of notions which include a capacity for expressing our true nature; or achieving our full potential; or feeling (as the French would say) comfortable in our own skin; or gaining in self-awareness so that we have a pretty accurate understanding of our own motives and feelings. Now, this is all good, positive and laudable (dare we say it?) New Age stuff. But if we step outside of the discourse for a moment, we might find ourselves compelled to ask the question: Is it always desirable that *every* individual should become their authentic self? We're not necessarily talking about extreme cases, such as those we explored in the previous chapter, where an individual's idea of self-fulfilment is to become a homicidal maniac; but what if you as a mentor began to suspect that a learner's "authentic self" encompasses sociopathic tendencies or a single-minded obsession with material gain? What if Gill, instead of becoming "more human," decides to become "more authentically herself" and turns out not to be just an old softy at heart, but even more of an unapproachable ratbag than she had previously allowed herself to be?

BECOMING LESS HUMAN? SOME RESERVATIONS ABOUT EASY-FIX THEORIES

The point here is that it may be a mistake to assume that personal change and self-fulfilment will always or inevitably indicate a move in a positive direction. Mentors in fairytales and in space operas may never have to face up to this realization; but as real life mentors we probably do need to. We need to be wary, too, about confusing *real/authentic* with *self-centred/take-me-or-leave-me*. For example, you might be forgiven for thinking that the colleague who says: "I'm just a down to earth person, me. I just tell it how I see it. And I know I do have issues sometimes about possessiveness and control," is exhibiting honesty and self-knowledge. But it's quite possible that what they're actually saying is, "This is how I am, chum. And I don't intend to change. So you'd better take me on my own terms or not at all."

The way that we approach personal change, either as mentor or learner, will depend to a large extent on how easy we think it is to achieve it. Are human beings infinitely plastic creatures, adjusting their preferences and behaviors at the drop of a hat, or are our values, beliefs and therefore our responses, ingrained over years of experience and conditioning, like the rings of a tree, and just as stubbornly resistant to alteration?[2] We should perhaps also reflect that, for some people in society this journey towards self-actualization, towards becoming the person you want to be, is enormously difficult and fraught with obstacles. For others, with the benefits of a good education and social advantage, it may feel more within their grasp, if still somewhat of a challenge. Some of these easy theories of self-actualization and self-help may be seen, by their very nature, as leaving certain sections of society out of account. So where does this leave us as mentors? Do we perhaps need a broader and more inclusive view of personal change and self-actualization? This is a question we shall return to.

HOW PERFECT DOES THE MENTOR HAVE TO BE?

If the learner is willing and capable of working towards the goal of positive personal change, to what extent do mentors themselves need to be "together" and self-fulfilled? Although some mentors – Captain Jean-Luc Picard for one – are overwhelmingly wonderful in every way, some, like Honest John in the Pinocchio story, are far from perfect. He is a bit of a showman. His milieu is the theatre; and this theatrical aspect of the character warns us at once that his concern is with acting and masks and make believe. These are fairly obvious clues that "Honest" John isn't very honest at all, particularly in terms of self-knowledge (which, after all, is mainly a matter of being honest with ourselves). There's nothing much about him that is authentic, and so it's not surprising that he's unable to provide effective mentoring and support for Pinocchio on the puppet's quest for self-fulfilment.

In fact, there are three major misleading ideas encouraged by Honest John, each of which presents an altogether superficial or inauthentic approach to personal development and aspirational goal-setting. They are:

- *Misleading idea # 1: Success can be achieved without hard work.* According to Honest John, hard work is a waste of time. Success is achieved by luck, or through the sheer foolishness of others. In this, he seems to be of one mind with the authors of all those self-improvement books currently cluttering up the bookshops with titles such as, *Lose Ten Stone Without Moving From Your Couch,* or *Make a Million Dollars By Sitting On The Sofa and Picking Your Nose.* We've discussed the effort that both Data and Pinocchio had to put in on their way to achieving their goals. Any mentor who tells a learner that hard work isn't necessary for personal change is at best misguided and at worst – like Honest John – a charlatan.
- *Misleading idea # 2: Education and learning are unimportant.* Honest John wouldn't even bother to hold a book the right way up. His advice is that education is irrelevant. While sometimes this might just be the case, it is certainly misleading to deny the importance that learning – and *the willingness to learn* – play in the process of self-development and personal change. Pinocchio doesn't make progress until he accepts that he has things to learn; and Data's appetite for learning seems insatiable. Effective mentors never underplay the importance of learning.

- *Misleading idea # 3: Acclaim is a valid end in itself.* It's enough, says Honest John, to see your name in lights, to simply be famous. It needn't involve being good at anything, achieving anything of note, or employing any talent – all those things which wisdom and experience tell us are the genuine key to fulfilment. No, says Honest John. Not necessary. Fame and acclaim are all that matter. This mindset is sometimes referred to now as the "Big Brother syndrome," after the TV reality show where contestants set their sights on being famous for being...well, famous. The ultimate aim here is to be "papped" (followed and photographed by the paparazzi). Good mentors are, of course, able to point out clearly the difference between being "papped" and achieving some degree of personal growth.

THE GOOD ENOUGH MENTOR AND THE QUEST FOR AUTHENTICITY: *EDUCATING RITA*

The subject of flawed mentors brings us neatly to Dr. Frank Bryant, played by Michael Caine in the film of Willy Russell's play, *Educating Rita*. He is a university lecturer who finds himself in the dual role of tutor and mentor to Rita. She is a good-hearted working class woman and Open University student of literature, played by Julie Walters. Dr. Frank certainly has his flaws. One of them is drink. Another is his attitude of disillusion and cynicism, fuelled by a failed marriage and his disappointment at not achieving his own life goal which was to become a successful poet. Into his life comes Rita, a hairdresser, who has chosen study as a way of avoiding the pressure on her from her husband, Denny, and from her wider family, to settle down to domestic life and have a baby. She and Frank come from two quite different worlds: hers is one of back streets, terraced houses, corner pubs and tightly defined expectations about gender roles; while his social circle consists of largely superficial, moderately affluent and "cultured" acquaintances who indulge themselves in fine wines and extra-marital affairs. At first Rita, dazzled by the superficial glamour, aspires to Frank's world. She adopts him as a mentor, and seeks to change herself in order to conform to what she sees as the rules, expectations and behaviors of this privileged and cultured set. In the process she finds herself in a sort of no-man's-land where she still does not quite fit into Frank's set, but has become distanced from her own family and her original "working class" roots. Her alienation and isolation are captured in the film when she is shown trying – and failing – to fit in at Frank's party, and then going on to join her parents in her local pub where, too, she is gradually becoming an outsider.

PERSONAL CHANGE V. SUPERFICIAL TINKERING

The trouble is that, in trying to conform to Frank's world, Rita is being no more authentically herself than she would be if she gave up her aspirations for learning and self-improvement and settled down under pressure to have a house full of kids. The changes that she makes to her appearance and her behavior are merely superficial. For example, her real name is "Susan," but she changes it to "Rita" when she becomes a student, after an author whose work she admires.

She tells Frank she's not a Susan any more. This is a statement about personal *identity*. But a change of name alone is surely not enough (although The Artist Formerly Known as Prince may not agree with us there), and should certainly not be mistaken for genuine personal change. Personal change is not about adopting a new identity, but about gaining self-understanding in order to become more fully ourselves. Rita changes her style of dress and her style of conversation, and – to some extent – her accent, all in an effort to change who she is; but in Frank's view she is simply exchanging one socially stereotyped role – that of working class woman – for another – that of privileged middle-class student. She can now "play the game," but has repressed those qualities he first admired in her: her originality and spontaneity and enthusiasm. This "new" Rita is simply a set of affectations. She has done some tinkering, but has not undergone any real, meaningful, developmental change. She has shown that she can *learn*, certainly; but what she has learned is simply to imitate the outward behavior of others. In order to genuinely change and develop, she will need to learn about *herself*. Despite his obvious flaws, Frank knows this. He feels that what he has created through his mentoring is a monster. Just like Dr. Frankenstein's reanimated collection of body parts, Rita is now neither wholly herself nor authentically the self she is capable of becoming. The acid test for Frank is that Rita now is unable to see his poetry for the third rate nonsense it really is. (Remember the important part that an understanding of literature played in Data's project to understand what it means to be fully and authentically human?) When Rita mouths platitudes about Frank's poems she is demonstrating a failure to trust her own judgement; a failure to be authentically herself. She is saying what she thinks is expected from her. She is courting approval and using flattery rather than speaking from the heart. In this sense she has not undergone any meaningful change, but has simply tinkered with aspects of the face she presents to the world.

And yet, on some level, Rita does understand the significance and meaning of personal change. She reflects on the unrealistic expectations of some of the women who come into the hairdressing salon where she works; and of one unprepossessing woman in particular who brings in a picture of Princess Di, believing that if she adopts the same hairdo as Diana she will somehow achieve the same glamour and grace. Rita recognizes that this is expecting too much; that for real change to take place it has to happen from the inside. And Frank, too, despite his drinking and his cynicism and his hollow life-style, is not totally self-deluded. He knows that he is no poet, that this is not where his talents lie. And he sees clearly that Rita is learning the wrong lessons from him. He recognizes that she has taken a wrong turning on her journey, just as Rita herself recognizes the futility of her client's efforts to "become" Princess Di. This glimmer of self-knowledge which each possesses means that Frank and Rita, despite their flaws and the wrong turnings they've taken, are able to act to some extent as mentors to each other. They each enable the other to recognize the superficial masks and goals they've adopted to present to the world; and their relationship forces each of them to look inwards and learn something about who they really are and what they really want. Ultimately, though, it is Rita, at first apparently the one most constrained by her circumstances, who is able to use this self-knowledge effectively in order to make positive choices about her goals. Rita is also better at building Frank's self esteem than he is at building hers; *and* she is a more attentive listener. Frank, on the other hand, resents Rita's growing independence from him and eventually does something that's certainly best avoided by mentors, which is to fall in love with the learner!

Nevertheless, although he's not a particularly good mentor Frank is, in a sense, *good enough*. At the end of the film we feel that both characters have gained a degree of self-knowledge, but that it is Rita who is comfortable with what she has learned, and she who has achieved a degree of peace with herself. Their relationship, despite its setbacks does illustrate the *mutual benefit* that can be gained by mentor and learner. It serves as an example, too, of how the learner can outgrow the mentor, and how the nature of the relationship has then to change – to that of friends or colleagues – if it is to continue in any positive way.

CHOICE, IDENTITY, CHANGE AND LOSS

We have already seen in our summary of the Pinocchio story that one of the key factors in the quest for self-fulfilment is *choice*. In *Educating Rita*, both Rita and Frank feel trapped by the circumstances of their lives and by the expectations of others. It is this feeling which makes Rita want to break out of the identity which she fears is being forced upon her – that of traditional wife and mother with no aspirations outside the home – and to discover what else she could be. She decides to stop being Susan and start being Rita. Unlike Frank, she makes a choice, a courageous one, to begin the process of change. And, even though her first efforts lead her up a blind alley, she hangs on to that sense of agency and free will, and makes the choice in the end to work towards her exams, which tells us that she is now able to set herself realistic goals and feel confident to pursue them.

Recognizing that we have a choice engenders a sense of empowerment, *however limited that choice may be.* Data, for example, cannot choose to be human, but he can choose to learn about what being human means. Pinocchio is luckier. He *can* choose to be human, and does. Rita chooses to find out more about who she is capable of becoming, and pursues this goal within the constraints that inevitably limit the choices she makes. But, of course, making a choice can often involve loss as well as gain, as we saw when Rita became stranded between her two worlds. And some losses we can readily recognize, as in this conversation between Gill and her mentor, Meena:

GILL: It's been an amazing few months. I think I've hit every target I was given when I was appointed in January. Every single one!

MEENA: These are targets set by the organization?

GILL: Yep. These are the ones I was told needed to be met. And bingo! Job done.

MEENA: And what about your own targets – is there anything you feel you'd personally like to aim for?

GILL: Same thing. Getting the job done. And I have to say, I reckon I've succeeded against all the odds. It's been like pushing a boulder up a hill sometimes. My team act like some sort of reluctant chain gang, shuffling along. Unenthusiastic. Looking put out when I ask for a bit of extra effort.

MEENA: Is that how you see them?

GILL: Well, honestly, it's like pulling teeth.

MEENA: Is that how they see you, do you think?

GILL: What? Scary dentist? Slave driver?

MEENA: Either.

GILL: Probably both. Oh dear. It's a shame, isn't it? I suppose it would be nicer to feel that we were really working as a team. I mean, we were all the same team originally. And then I got this promotion, and since then it's been a question of me on one side and them on the other. You know that old saying: "It's lonely at the top"? I'm their team leader now, so I can't afford to be too friendly.

MEENA: Why do you say that?

GILL: Well, I can't. Can I?.......... Or are you saying you think I should be?

MEENA: You know, I may be wrong, but you sound almost as though you regret this distance that's sprung up?

GILL: I suppose I do in a way. It does feel a bit sad sometimes. We were all quite a happy team once....

Is this a sign of Gill about to become "more human"? Well, who knows? But what we can see from this conversation is that her *choice* to take a promotion has not come without its cost. She now finds herself friendless and isolated, and is evidently feeling nostalgic about the time she was part of a happy team. It's also clear that she sees *goals* as things that are set by the organization. When her mentor asks her about personal goals, Gill doesn't think in terms of self fulfilment or personal change, or any other kind of goal she might set for herself. She thinks only of "getting the job done." This suggests that she doesn't see herself as having real choices. In taking on the identity of "leader" she has accepted uncritically the platitude about it being lonely at the top (or about three rungs up, which is probably where Gill is in reality) and so assumes she has no option but to distance herself from her erstwhile friends. So, at least we know now the reason she has adopted the behavior that her team see as not very human. Gill is unable to combine the role of leader with being authentically herself. But perhaps this conversation with her mentor will jump-start a process of genuine change.

COST TO OTHERS

It is not only the traveller on the road to self-fulfilment themselves who must pay the cost of life changes and choices made. Rita's husband, Denny, is left angry and hurt by the change in his wife. He feels he has lost the happy-go-lucky girl he married. Frank, too, fears for what will happen to himself when Rita's trajectory takes her eventually out of his orbit. Frank's question is: if he tries to change himself, to reform, how will he keep up the effort when she – as she inevitably will – moves on? We have only to think of the parent and spouse who deserts their family in order to "find themselves"; or the writer who shuts out loved ones in order to concentrate on their creative goal; or the clever youngster – the high academic achiever – who finds they have less and less in common with (and less and less time for) their proud but bewildered parents. This has nothing in common with Gill's quote about it being "lonely at the top." This is about the often inevitable collateral damage which results when a choice is made to pursue personal change and self-fulfilment.

GOALS OR DREAMS?
RATSO AND THE MIDNIGHT COWBOY

What happens, though when the choices we can make are severely limited, by poverty or by social exclusion? We've seen how Rita and Frank were able to help one another towards becoming more authentically themselves in a relationship which could at one stage be described as mutual mentoring. In this final section of the chapter we're going to look at another classic film in which a pair of characters support one another on their journey, but with a grimmer and less certain outcome. *Midnight Cowboy*, a John Schlesinger film from 1969, based on the 1965 novel by James Leo Herlihy, tells the story of two characters who encounter each other while each is in pursuit of his own version of the American Dream. As the lyrics of the title song suggests, the dreams of both of them involve escape from the mundane world and the start of a newer, better life. For the disabled, tubercular and impoverished Rizzo (nicknamed Ratso for his streetwise ways) the dream is a fairly literal one. He wants to get to Florida. If he can get to Florida, so his reasoning goes, he will feel fit and healthy and comfortable at last. John Buck, the Midnight Cowboy of the title (who is, in fact, no cowboy at all) dreams of living the comfortable life by becoming a successful male prostitute and making his fortune from selling himself to rich, middle-aged women. Both characters are full of hope for the success of their dreams, and even though both have clearly had difficult early lives in which they have been victims of poverty, violence and, in Rizzo's case, serious illness, this does not dim their optimism. But sadly, John Buck's attempts to become a gigolo lead to degradation and violence; and Rizzo's health deteriorates to the point where it becomes obvious that he is dying. Still supporting each other's optimism, they get on a bus for Florida and comfort each other with talk of how good life will be when they get there. But during the long journey Rizzo dies in John Buck's arms.

In this grim story of Rizzo and John Buck we see echoed several of the themes we've been discussing in this chapter, but this time presented in a haunting, minor key. For example:

- *Goals and dreams:* Rizzo's and John's goals are unrealistic. The Florida sun will not cure Rizzo's TB nor his maimed leg. John will never make it as a high class gigolo, because it is not rich women who find his cowboy persona attractive, but gay men. Their goals are not goals in the sense that Rita and Pinocchio and you and I might formulate them. In fact, they are dreams; and, more specifically, they are *dreams of escape* from the grim reality of their day-to-day existence. They are not goals connected with personal change and development, but daydreams which function more like a comfort blanket. Here is where easy theories about "self-actualization" fall down. For people like Rizzo and John the only urgent goals are survival and relief from pain. And because their dreams of escape are to a large extent self-deluding, they are really just another form of self-limiting belief, because they serve as an excuse to avoid formulating realistic goals which will actually move them forward. Much earlier in the chapter we referred to the android Data's desire to be more like a human as being more of a dream than a goal. But there is a major difference between Data's dream and the dreams of Rizzo and John: Where theirs are *delusional and self-limiting*, Data's is *aspirational and inspirational*. In other words, the android's dream encourages personal change, learning, and a movement towards self-fulfilment, while theirs serve the opposite purpose.

- *Identity and authenticity:* There is an irony in the naming of both main characters in *Midnight Cowboy*. The eponymous John Buck is not a real cowboy, although he dresses and presents himself as one; and Rizzo doesn't want to be called Ratso, although this is the name by which he's referred to throughout most of the film. In other words, what the world sees is not the "real" them; and it's fairly clear that neither of them is sure about his own identity. We think here of Rita, who started out as Susan but wanted a new name for her new self. Or Pinocchio, who was not a real boy. Rita grows into her new name, eventually; and Pinocchio becomes a real boy. But poor John Buck and Rizzo, from their disadvantaged position, never do make that leap to become authentically themselves. Although they leave their Cowboy and Ratso personas behind at the very end, and formulate the more realistic goal of simply reaching Florida, they are still fooling themselves with the idea that Florida sunshine will solve all their problems, as Rizzo lies dying in John's arms.
- *Mutual mentoring: bringing out the best in each other:* Some might argue that these two characters simply lead each other even further into delusion and squalor, as John learns from Rizzo how to cheat and steal, an engagement with crime which ends with him committing a serious assault. But we can certainly read their relationship in another way because, although both of them are flawed, they do eventually, like Frank and Rita, draw out positive qualities in one another, such as loyalty and friendship and tenderness. This change towards the direction of *virtue* was something we saw in Pinocchio's journey to self-fulfilment. And they do begin to *learn* from their experiences, leaving the corruption of the city behind them.

JOURNEYS, REAL AND METAPHORICAL

John and Rizzo's journey is a real one, their mode of transport a Greyhound bus. Like the other characters we have discussed in this chapter, they are travelling. What makes their journey different, we would suggest, is that it is in the end undertaken as an escape – from the reality of squalor, violence and death; whereas the others are on a journey of discovery or a quest which is about personal change and self-fulfilment. The others make a choice; but Rizzo and John find themselves out of choices and are, in effect, on the run. This is where we see the limitations of glib theories about routes to self-fulfilment. They simply ignore the extreme circumstances in which some sections of society live. Compare the fairytale of Pinocchio who, after some false starts, is on a journey of which each stage marks a stage in his development from mere puppet to human boy. Rita's journey is a metaphorical one of self-discovery. She has a false start, too, but later gets into her stride as she gains in confidence and self-understanding. Data's journey is to "boldly go" and seek out new worlds. He's not on the run from anything, either; and his journey takes him not only into the depths of space but also into the depths of the human spirit.

SUMMARY

All the four stories we have considered in this chapter have dealt in one way or another with the idea of a journey or a quest. As mentor, part of our role is to become facilitator of this journey. To carry out our role effectively we need to consider four crucial questions:

- What will provide the best chance of the learner achieving change or fulfilment?
- What might scupper their chances?
- To what extent is the theory of self-actualization acceptable and workable in the learner's current circumstances?
- What might be the costs to the learner of personal change or self-fulfilment?

If we apply these questions to our four stories we come up with a range of views about personal change, some of them conflicting. For Pinocchio, wishes can come true. Change is difficult and costs effort, but a complete transformation is possible. His story in this way is an embodiment of the American Dream. It seems to promise that, however severe our initial disadvantage, we can become whatever we aspire to be. The story of the Midnight Cowboy, on the other hand, presents us with answers which are far grimmer and, we would suggest, much more realistic. Ratso and the Cowboy are so damaged and impeded by their disadvantaged pasts and their present impoverished circumstances that real change may be impossible, however devoutly it is wished for. Their struggles with the impossibility of gaining any real control over their lives gives the lie to the shiny promises of the American Dream. The journey of the android, Data, however, presents the slightly more optimistic view that, although we are limited by our intrinsic selves, we can nevertheless within those limits achieve some degree of change; although it will cost us a great deal of persistence and hard work. And Rita's story, while also suggesting that we can, with effort, break free of our past and our limited horizons, poses the further, important question of "why?" Her transformation reminds us not only that there is a high price to pay for change, but also that we should be clear about what motivates us, and that the change is an authentic one. For us as mentors, the way we behave within the mentoring process will depend to a great extent on which of these views most closely aligns with our own in the context of what we know of the learner.

REFERENCES

[1]Maslow, A. (1970). *Motivation and Personality* (2nd Ed.). New York: Harper and Row.
[2]Smail, D. (1987). *Taking Care – An Alternative to Therapy*, London: J.M. Dent & Sons.
[3]Egan, G. (2007). *The Skilled Helper* (8th Ed). Belmont, CA: Thomson.

Television, Films and Books

Disney, W. (Producer). (1940). *Pinocchio* [Motion picture]. Burbank, CA: Disney. (Adapted from the original fairy tale, *Pinocchio – Tale of a Puppet* by Carlo Collodi [1883]).

Gilbert. L. (Director), & Russell, W. (Writer). (1983). *Educating Rita* [Motion picture]. UK: Acorn Pictures.

Roddenberry, G. (Producer/director). (1987 to 1994). *Star Trek: The Next Generation* {Television series]. Los Angeles, CA: Paramount Television.

Schlesinger, J. (Director). (1969). *Midnight Cowboy* [Motion picture]. Century City, CA: United Artists. (Based on the novel of the same name by James Leo Herlihy [1965]).

CHAPTER 6

THE ENEMY WITHIN, OR JUST A CRITICAL FRIEND?

The Subversive Mentor or Transformation Through Subversion, Humour and Tough Love

---

THE PRIME OF MISS JEAN BRODIE

An Edinburgh street in 1932, and Jean Brodie, a teacher at Marcia Blaine School, cycles to work to start a new term. The opening of Ronald Neame's 1969 film, adapted by Jay Presson Allen from her own play of Muriel Spark's novel, introduces us to one of the most intriguing and contradictory mentors to appear in film or in print.

This is the story of Miss Jean Brodie, a woman "in her prime." It concerns an unconventional teacher with strongly-held and radical beliefs about the education of her impressionable young charges, and the effect that her presence and her methods have upon the staff and the pupils of the conservative girls school where she has worked for some years. Played in the film by Maggie Smith, in an award-winning tour de force, Miss Brodie steeps her young "gels" in the glories of Italian art, the attractions of Mussolini's fascist movement, and the details of her own tragic love affair with a young soldier killed in the final days of World War One. What she skips over in rather more cursory fashion are such aspects of the compulsory curriculum as science, mathematics and the Battle of Flodden. Eventually this highly personal and somewhat eccentric learning agenda, long-suspected by the school authorities, but cunningly hidden with the connivance of Brodie's students, proves her downfall and she is forced to resign from Marcia Blaine in disgrace. It is this deliberate undermining of authority and refusal to conform to the norms and behaviors expected by the educational establishment, in the guise of Miss McKay, the head-teacher, which define Jean Brodie's approach to her vocation and which forms the focus of this chapter. Although first and foremost a teacher, Jean Brodie acts very much as mentor to her inner circle of favoured pupils, "the Brodie set," and she undoubtedly has an influence on their social, political and spiritual development that goes further than most teacher-pupil relationships.

If part of the mentor's role is to help others bring about change in the way they think, work and see the world, to what extent should a mentor subvert the accepted ways of doing and looking at things, question the status quo, and undermine so-called authority, in order to best serve their learners? How far should the subversive mentor go, and what are the dangers inherent in taking this to excess? In all her mess of contradictions, self-delusion, romantic high-mindedness and hypocrisy, Jean Brodie illustrates some of the best and the worst aspects of the subversive mentor, and provides us with an entertaining case study by which to examine some of the questions above.

THE BEST OF MISS JEAN BRODIE

In the book, Sandy, a leading light in the "Brodie set" and the pupil who ultimately betrays her, is forced to admit that, in hindsight, Jean Brodie's inability to see her own glaring flaws as both teacher and mentor did *not* prevent her from having some positive impact on her students. It is significant that the Brodie girls, with the exception of poor Mary MacGregor, were among the brightest in the school. In fact it is partly due to this that the Headmistress has such a difficult job discrediting her troublesome member of staff. It would appear, on the face of it, that Jean Brodie is at least doing something right.

She clearly considers her role as being partly to compensate for what she sees as the petrifying effect of the school's small-mindedness and dedication to the status quo. She refuses to be constrained by the demands of the curriculum when, in her eyes, an appreciation of art, music and beauty is every bit as important to the girls' broader development. She encourages the girls to question the existing order, by being openly critical of the school authorities, and society's assumptions about the merits of teamwork, clubs and societies. (She takes a rather cruel pop at the Girl Guides in particular.) She uses stories and personal experience to capture the young pupils' imagination, and to bring to life issues of love, loss, heroism and dedication to a cause. Like all schoolchildren, they might invent funny stories about their teacher, and giggle behind her back, but there is no doubt that Miss Brodie's students are captivated by her and by her lessons.

She tells her headmistress that she doesn't believe in talking down to children. Her stated views on education, based on the Latin root meaning a "leading out" of what is there already, would find favour with most mentors, seeking to help their learners unearth and make sense of their own intrinsic knowledge. By contrast, the hope of the exasperated Head, Miss MacKay, that this dangerously unconventional teacher might deign to actually "put something in" once in a while, might be entirely understandable in the circumstances, but represents a view of learning which is inimical to the mentoring process. In Jean Brodie's world, by exposing her girls to art and culture, regardless of its relevance to the curriculum, she is stimulating their interest in all that is fine and beautiful. They might not know what the capital of Finland is or be able to solve a quadratic equation, but they could express a view on the merits of a Giotto painting, (even if this view was generally that of Miss Brodie herself). She believes in people's potential for greatness, and although this manifests itself partly in the fantasies she constructs about what her students are each destined to achieve, it also drives her constantly to raise her pupils' aspirations and to encourage them to make their mark. She tells them that they are all "heroines" and tries to instill in them the desire to have opinions, believe in something and dedicate their lives to some cause.

So one would have to recognize that there are some telling examples here of behavior all mentors aim to emulate:

- A focus on *drawing out knowledge,* rather than inserting it.
- Encouragement of *continuous learning* and personal growth.
- Introduction of *new perspectives* and a *broadening of horizons* and aspirations.
- An assumption that *every learner has the potential to be successful* in some field, provided they are prepared to dedicate themselves to it.
- An impetus towards questioning the status quo and thinking critically about so-called received wisdom. A *willingness to challenge authority* and look at alternative interpretations of the world around us, with a view to finding new ways of doing things and thinking about things.

It is in particular this latter point which we are interested in exploring further, concerning as it does the potentially beneficial role of subversion in the change and learning process.

WHY IS SUBVERSION NECESSARY?
THE COMMENTATORS' VIEW

There is no doubt that Jean Brodie is a hugely subversive influence in Marcia Blaine School. The approach she takes to her job challenges convention, as does the impact she has both on her pupils and on her male colleagues, the two rivals for her affections: Mr. Lloyd, the flamboyant art teacher and Mr. Lowther, the mild-mannered music master. She is not called "the dangerous Miss Brodie" for nothing. She persuades pupils to collude with her in deceiving the school authorities about her disregard for the curriculum. She keeps a math equation on the blackboard, and asks the class to hold up history books while she recounts stories of her holiday visits to Italian centres of culture. She openly tells pupils of her struggles with the headmistress and the latter's plotting to get rid of her. She encourages her charges to reflect on subjects much broader than the set curriculum and jeopardizes their exam success in the process. In these days of national curriculum, studying obsessively to exams and constant testing of schoolchildren, it is quite possible that this aspect of Jean Brodie would be as lionized by frustrated teachers as it would be demonized by results-obsessed parents. But, for all its faults, does this kind of subversion have a part to play in learning and change, and, by extension, in mentoring?

The view has been expressed that the purpose of mentoring, in schools specifically, must extend to changing existing cultural norms, if it is really to succeed in transforming teacher and student performance. In order for mentoring to be more than a mere training and induction "add-on" for new staff, this "countercultural" role must be acknowledged and the subversive nature of mentoring exploited.[1] In a similar vein, the benefit of subversive change is being recognized in other kinds of organization too. Top-down change "programs" are being questioned in favour of the unfortunately-named "bottom-up" strategies. Such employee engagement strategies might include, for example, identifying and disseminating isolated pockets of good practice. Significantly, researchers at Cranfield School of Management, Martin Clarke and Mike Meldrum, cite several case studies of this kind of change where subversion was a key attribute of the change agent.[2] The argument is that, in order to create significant change, organizational norms have to be challenged and the existing order subverted, regardless of the discomfort caused to those not recognizing the need for improvement. Such an approach requires a change agent who can stand outside the organization, its prevailing culture, history and norms of behavior. There are obvious parallels here with the way a good mentor helps facilitate individual change. Making reference to William Bridges' work on personal transition, Laurent Daloz writes eloquently of the need to stop simply believing things and to cast doubt on our assumptions about the world in order to become "critically reflective" and thus think and learn for ourselves. This means welcoming that unsettling sense of previous "knowledge" being swept away as a necessary part of enlightenment; something which Buddhist thinkers have apparently likened to the bottom falling out of a bucket of water.[3]

This makes sense. If all a mentor does is loyally subscribe to the cultural, behavioral and managerial norms of whatever environment he or she is working in, then the potential for change must be severely limited. Indeed these very norms may well be the barriers to self-development against which the learner is struggling. Let us suppose the organization subscribes to a set of values which may lead to unnecessarily high levels of stress, alienation, frustration of ambition and the squashing of creativity, innovation and initiative. A mentor who simply accepts these conditions or, worse still, allows themselves to become complicit in them, will certainly not rock the boat, but is pretty unlikely to generate much learning or change either. In which case, a mentor is more useful if they can not only preserve an open mind about the taken for granted assumptions that prevail in the mentoring "environment," but also challenge and question those assumptions, and encourage their learners to do likewise.

All well and good, but I suspect this may sound a bit scary if you are the person responsible for the mentoring scheme in a large organization. It is one thing for a mentor to be subversive and undermining of the status quo in a one-off mentor-learner relationship, but what about where the contract involves a third party: the school/hospital/company who are probably footing the bill for the whole thing? Well, it comes down to an omelette and eggs argument really. If an organization does not want people to question what is going on around them and prefers to maintain existing ways of operating as sacrosanct, then it can certainly use mentoring to do this. However, the result is more likely to be indoctrination than real learning and a great opportunity for innovation and improvement will have been missed. For those organizations willing to take the risk of opening up their cultures and traditions to a bit of sceptical examination, there are a number of circumstances where this kind of "subversive mentoring" may be very constructive. Let us look at some of them:

- The mentoring scheme may actually have been *designed to question assumptions and undermine the status quo.* (Examples would include reverse mentoring and diversity schemes). Alternatively it may be aimed deliberately at shifting the balance of power (e.g. schemes to empower service user representatives in the public sector).
- The *organizational norms may be the barrier* to the learner achieving the goals they have set themselves. Unless they learn to question these they cannot make progress.

- The learner may be *lacking the self-confidence to develop a productive relationship with an intimidating colleague/boss* and this involves helping them overcome their fear of the other person by undermining the awe-inspiring image they have created.
- The learner needs help *finding ways to influence their boss or their colleagues* more successfully in order to achieve their goals.
- To unlock the creativity needed to make a necessary transformation, a certain amount of *playing around and experimentation is required* and some "sacred cows" inevitably have to be abandoned.

According to Joseph Kessels in his work on knowledge management[4], the school curriculum, which Jean Brodie treats with such disdain, is mirrored in organizations. This "corporate curriculum," essentially the organization's learning environment, may be "closed" or "open." Where the curriculum is "closed" the content and outcomes of learning are tightly controlled, and knowledge is essentially certain and defined. (Think back to our mediaeval monks in *The Name of the Rose.*) Where the "corporate curriculum" is open, such boundaries are not assumed and learning can be the result of uncertainty, change and paradox. In simple terms, an organization's attitude to this "corporate curriculum" will determine how comfortable it is with the idea of subversion as part of mentoring and change. Just how worried should we be about the possible dangers of the subversive mentor, and what might the consequences be of getting this wrong?

THE WORST OF MISS JEAN BRODIE –
WHAT CAN GO WRONG?

So far, in discussing how Jean Brodie plays fast and loose with the core curriculum at Marcia Blaine, we have chosen to present this as a broadening of the pupils' education through the introduction of topics such as art, politics and her own love life; whereas in truth, what the girls actually receive is a different kind of *limited* curriculum: one limited by what Jean Brodie considers to be important. Sadly, whilst Miss Brodie's pupils are exposed to new knowledge, this is often *instead* of the usual subjects, rather than in addition to them. What is more, much as their minds may be opened to new experience by their teacher's tales of her holidays in Italy, what this amounts to is merely another form of indoctrination. Miss Brodie asks her class who is the greatest Italian painter, but this is not the start of an open-minded debate. She greets the answer Leonardo da Vinci with the curt reply that this is incorrect and the answer is Giotto, because he is her "favorite." Much of the film and the book's comedy and satirical edge derive from this yawning gulf between what Jean Brodie deludes herself she is doing and what she actually does. She purports to despise such bastions of conformity and uniformity as the Girl Guides, but actively seeks to convert her pupils to the cause of fascism as exemplified by Mussolini, Franco and even (in the book at least) Adolf Hitler. Her abhorrence of the concept of "team spirit" and her championing of the cause of the individual is hard to square with images of identically-clad fascisti marching through the streets of Rome. It is a clever metaphor for how Miss Brodie replaces one conformity with another. Her casual attitude to traditional school subjects is not about freedom of thought; in fact far from it. She hectors her pupils as to what they should think and do, rather like a fascist dictator herself, a fact that does not escape Mr. Lloyd who mocks her for treating the "Brodie set" like her own personal "fascisti." She even goes so far as to prescribe in some detail exactly what futures lie in store for her girls, pigeon-holing them with little thought for their own wishes and desires, and generally proving wildly inaccurate. She predicts that Jenny (Rose in the novel) will be a great lover and artistic muse, even trying to engineer a love affair between her and the art teacher Mr. Lloyd. But in the end it is Sandy who has an affair with Lloyd. Sandy, who Jean Brodie has down for a career as a spy, is supposed to be intellectual and rather plain, something achieved in the film, in true cinematic style, by giving the pretty (and award-winning) actress, Pamela Franklin, some Arthur Askey glasses to wear.

Furthermore, the "dangerous" Miss Brodie does not stop at imposing her own wistful, romantic fantasies on her impressionable young pupils. She actually manipulates others into living out these fantasies in shockingly inappropriate ways. She is unsuccessful at coaxing Jenny/Rose into Mr. Lloyd's bed, but does actually succeed in persuading Mary McGregor (Joyce Emily in the novel) to go and fight in the Spanish Civil War, giving her specific travel instructions and even the requisite money. Only after the poor girl's death does she discover that the none-too-bright student was actually headed off to fight for the Republicans *against* Brodie's beloved Franco. Far from "leading out" knowledge and ideas, Jean Brodie spends most of her time inserting them with the clipped rapidity of a fascisti's machine gun. The one thing she does *not* encourage her pupils to question is her. In fact so convinced is she of her own legitimacy that she is unable to see the damage she has done and accept responsibility even up to the very end.

So here we have a vivid illustration, not only of the good that can come from subverting and challenging conventional wisdom, but also the considerable dangers inherent in this. Miss Brodie is insufficiently self-aware to recognize how she imposes her own answers and ideas at the expense of multiple options, how she influences the easily-led and vulnerable, how she implicates her learners in illicit activities which could put them in harm's way, how she lives vicariously through others, leaving them with all the risk, and how her challenge to authority damages the lives of those around her more than it enhances them. We can summarize these dangers, along with the benefits of subversion in Table 6.1.

So, in the end, Miss Jean Brodie's brand of subversion ends up looking more like the kind of destructive individualism that is unlikely, on the whole, to give a net benefit either to the individual learner or to the organization. What can we do to avoid this? Is it purely about self-awareness or the lack of it? If we remove the self-delusion from Jean Brodie, does this provide sufficient check against the potential risks of subversive mentoring? To begin to answer this question, let us look at another example of a subversive mentor, the grizzled and irascible, but undoubtedly self-aware, Dr. House.

HOUSE

The eponymous hero of David Shore's hit television series, played by Hugh Laurie, is another subversive presence in an institution which must abide by accepted rules, standards and codes of conduct. This time the organization is a hospital and the "hero" is a doctor; not just any doctor, of course, but the best diagnostician in the land. (He was also voted *second* sexiest doctor on television – an accolade to which one suspects the character would

TABLE 6.1. A Subversive Approach

Mentoring Can Help By	But It Also Carries the Risk of
Rejecting the status quo and organizational/cultural norms in favour of multiple realities and multiple options	**Challenge becoming reductive NOT additive.** The purpose of challenge is to generate options in addition to conventional thinking not replace the status quo with a different convention
Stimulating creativity and improvisation	**Answers replacing questions** – Mentors are there primarily to ask questions, not provide a different set of answers
Removing perceived barriers to a learner's growth and development **Introducing new and different perspectives** on an issue	**Inappropriate ideas filling the void** – When the certainties of received wisdom are removed, learners are vulnerable to other ideas/strategies which may or may not be helpful or constructive. The mentor has a responsibility to help learners navigate this suggestible state successfully
Encouraging play, experimentation and new ways of seeing the world **Challenging preconceptions and assumptions** about other people, to reduce fear, misunderstanding and prejudice	**Learner becoming the lab rat** – Without necessarily realizing it, mentors can use others to experiment with their own risky ideas or fantasies of success, leaving the learner to carry the consequences

have had a suitably caustic riposte.) House works at the fictional Princeton-Plainsboro Teaching Hospital, where he is Chief of Diagnostic Medicine. A curmudgeonly maverick, he is assisted by a team of young doctors eager to learn from his mentoring, who actually spend most of their time being mocked, shouted at and generally ordered around. Where Jean Brodie is a deluded, if well-meaning fantasist, House is presented as something of a monster. He is arrogant, sarcastic and generally disregarding of all the normal conventions of social interaction. He routinely belittles colleagues, patients and subordinates, and treats pretty much everyone with contempt and scorn. Far from focusing on the needs of the learner, when House engages in question and answer sessions with his acolytes it is all about solving the puzzle. Patients for House seem to be no more than a collection of symptoms, designed to elude diagnosis, and cracking the code becomes a risk-all, high-stakes game. The thrill lies in pitting his highly trained diagnostic mind against a complex morass of symptoms, and winning. We are led to believe that, for House, the growth and development of the learner is subordinate to the solving of the mystery (as is the well-being of the patient). For this reason, he has been compared, as a character, to Sherlock Holmes dressed up in a lab coat (although actually House refuses to wear a white coat in case needy patients recognize him for a doctor).

Having said all of this, you cannot escape the feeling that, if you were a patient with a rare and mystifying condition, you would probably prefer to survive, albeit with your ego bent out of shape, at the hands of Dr. Gregory House, than die in the empathetic arms of a lesser diagnostician with a great bedside manner. In many ways he is the "anti-mentor," not because he ignores the accepted norms of the profession and institution in which he works, but because he subverts the most sacred tenets of mentoring itself. So, if as mentors we are really serious about challenging the status quo, might it be instructive to put aside some of mentoring's "sacred cows" and see what we might learn from the not-so-good doctor?

What exactly are the mentoring "rules" he subverts, and are there ever good reasons for questioning them?

- **"Unconditional positive regard"** – In this respect, House the maverick is nothing if not consistent. He has scant positive regard for anyone, and is no respecter of the time, space or expertise of others. He seems to assume that pretty much everyone is an idiot except for him, especially the patients. No mentor would last long with such an uncompromisingly misanthropic take on humanity, but equally we have already suggested in Chapter Four that unconditional positive regard may have its limits, and sometimes be at odds with the mentor's own values and moral code. How realistic is it to expect mentors to maintain this perspective at all times, and can learning and development still take place when it is absent?

- **Mutual trust** – House trusts no-one, and works on the principle that all patients lie about themselves. This is why pretty much every episode, the normal diagnostic process of taking a patient history must be supplemented by breaking into their home to seek clues. Without going as far as housebreaking, there are occasions when a mentor may decide to challenge the truthfulness of a statement or assumption because he or she feels that the learner is not being entirely honest, if only with themselves. Trust has to be earned by both parties, and we are not always conscious of our deceptions. So does a degree of scepticism have any role to play in mentoring and is taking everything a learner says at face value always the best way to help them?

- **Creating "safe space" by not judging** – Being mentored by House is like walking across a minefield in skis. Sooner or later, he will expose your ignorance and mock it mercilessly. Failing this, he will arbitrarily insult you in some way for getting the answer right. We all know mentoring works best in an environment in which the learner feels able to speak openly without fear of being judged or ridiculed. However, if we really want to stretch our learner by helping them to push the limits of their understanding and to think "outside the box" – something House does quite successfully, by the way – we might sometimes need to create and tolerate a degree of discomfort, and allow the learner to struggle or even fail. Is it a valid part of the mentor's role to occasionally create a "dangerous space"?

- **Do no harm** – Ironically, this is actually a medical axiom (part of the Hippocratic oath) which is frequently transposed from therapy to mentoring, and is clearly interpreted by House as "Do no harm *in the end.*" It is by no means unusual for the patients under House's "care" to be made significantly more ill by the unorthodox and often highly dangerous methods he employs to test his hypotheses (making one drink tequila shots to test liver function is one memorable example). Although they are generally saved against all the odds, they may suffer horribly in the process. Similarly, House subjects his learners to enormous risk by making them collude in ethically questionable and even downright illegal activities, with little or no thought to the consequences for their careers. He spends virtually one whole series getting applicants to fight, mistrust and betray each other for a job on his team. Of course, such a jaw-dropping lack of consideration creates great dramatic tension and not a little humour, but there is a serious lesson here too. Learning and discovery take place not in the well-charted territory of familiar ground but at the edges of our knowledge and our comfort zones. Is it not essential sometimes that mentors both take risks and encourage risk-taking in their learners if they want to evoke real transformation in thought and action?

- **Be open, honest and transparent** – The character of Dr. House is something of a paradox in this regard. In a way he is honest to the point of brutality. He refuses at one point even to allow a dying patient to have the comfort of believing in an afterlife. Likewise, he rarely spares the feelings of colleagues, patients or anyone else, if he has an opinion of them to share. But for Gregory House, the ends justify the means, and if that includes deceiving and manipulating others to get his own way, then he will engage in this just as enthusiastically.

OK, so maybe we shouldn't question all sacred cows......

As a drama, *House* only works if the audience retain some shred of sympathy and respect for the central character. This is partly achieved through his particular brand of excoriating sarcasm (he is very funny), and partly because we now and again sense that House does in fact want to save the patient as well as defeat the disease.

It also depends on Dr. House being the cleverest guy in the room and the wretched patient's only hope of survival. For a doctor who is in so many ways so very wrong, Gregory House is usually right. But the fact that his technical know-how is by and large unimpeachable, cannot make up for the fact that, in his obnoxious behavior, and flouting of moral, ethical and legal standards, he goes too far. Neither his expertise nor his self-awareness prevent the subversion being every bit as damaging as Jean Brodie's. This is primarily a matter of intent. House is simply not interested enough in developing others to be a good mentor to his staff. However misguided, Jean Brodie at least felt committed to her vocation as an educator.

SCRUBS – THE "RIGHT KIND OF SUBVERSION"?

So, while we are scrubbed up and in our surgical gowns, let us look at another medical mentoring relationship: this time that of Perry Cox and J.D. in the long-running comedy show, *Scrubs*. In many ways, Perry Cox, played by John C. McGinley, is a lot like Gregory House. He has a nice line in withering sarcasm, he gleefully teases and belittles his learner, John Dorian, (known as J.D. and played by Zach Braff), and he is no respecter of the authorities at Sacred Heart, the hospital where they both work. The dynamic of the relationship is neatly established from the very first episode. At their first meeting J.D., is informed that he is not allowed to talk when Perry is in the room. At their second meeting Perry tells J.D. that Dr. Kelso, the Chief of Medicine, is probably Satan. However, he cares enough to spot that J.D. is relying too heavily on nurses doing his procedures, and gently warns him that this will get him thrown out. By the end of the opening episode, for all his dyspeptic name-calling and sarcastic scorn, Cox has strengthened the young intern's confidence and expertise by urging J.D. to insert a chest tube all by himself, and take responsibility for his own patient.

In subsequent episodes Cox continues to address J.D. by a variety of girls' names, rail against the bureaucracy of hospital management (culminating in actually punching Bob Kelso), and generally react to J.D.'s puppy-like hero-worship with scathing verbal abuse. But in the process he manages to set a positive role model for professional dedication, making decisions on best available information and sticking to them, championing the cause of the patient, and recognizing the need to respect people's wishes about their own treatment. J.D. begins to learn that he cannot afford to become too emotionally attached to patients, because they must take responsibility for their own health, and in thinking he can "save" everyone he is bound to fail. He learns, above all, to differentiate between his own feelings and needs, and the best interests of the patient. All this he learns with the help of Perry Cox.

At this point, it is worth noting that one aspect of subversion embraced by all of our mentors so far, can prove a very positive force in a mentoring relationship; that is to say *humour*. We have mentioned already, in Chapter Three, how Sean uses humour to build rapport and create a "safe space" in his conversations with Will Hunting. But humour can also be used to subvert comfortable assumptions. In their popular and practical text-book, *Mentoring in Action*,[5] Megginson et al. cite a number of ways in which humour can do this:

- As a way of looking at the *brighter side* and gaining a *new perspective* on a difficult situation.
- By allowing the learner to understand their motives by accessing their "inner child."
- By enabling learners to recognize and examine *incongruities* in a relationship, situation or process.
- As a way of *reducing fear and anxiety* by introducing a sense of the ridiculous.

As a way of challenging well-established conventions and undermining taken-for-granted assumptions, humour proves an effective tool for Doctors House and Cox, but what is it that makes Perry's influence such a recognizably more positive one than Gregory's?

- *He has positive intent* – Although he sometimes works hard to hide it, Perry does genuinely care about his learner's development and about his patients, as well as about beating injury and disease. If he subverts hospital policy, it is in order to help a patient, rather than to prove he is right. Usually, if he teases J.D., it's because he recognizes that he has something to learn.

- *He is a good role model* – Knocking out the Chief of Medicine to one side, Cox is actually a pretty positive role model for J.D. He is competent, dedicated, good with patients, respectful of nursing staff and other colleagues, a realistic judge of human behavior, and clear-minded about ethical dilemmas and patient rights.
- *His mentoring matches his learner* – However brutal and sarcastic Perry Cox is towards J.D., and obviously this is exaggerated for comic effect, we understand that the thrust of this "tough love" approach is entirely appropriate. J.D. starts out highly dependent on nursing colleagues and senior staff, unable to make clear decisions, permanently seeking reassurance, and, in general, hopelessly ill-equipped for the emotionally challenging work of caring for the sick and dying. He drastically needs to toughen up, without losing his natural concern for patients, and, however exaggerated, Perry Cox's mix of tough love and strong positive role-modelling seem to do the job.

Dr. Cox uses subversion to question some of the organization's decisions about resourcing and patient care, and to ridicule those, such as Bob Kelso, whose actions he regards as self-serving and whose values undermine the way he believes medicine should be practiced. He also uses it to hold a mirror up to J.D., and help him to recognize when he is being a whiny, dependent do-gooder, rather than the pragmatic, confident, and decisive doctor that his patients need. However much J.D. values Dr. Cox's mentoring as an individual, from the organization's perspective he is, like both Jean Brodie and House, undermining and potentially dangerous. But, on balance, is he a force for good within the hospital or not?

Perhaps the problem here lies with the nature of the process itself. There is always the danger that reliance on individual development strategies like mentoring and coaching either encourage too many individual change agendas all pulling in different directions or become mere sterile tools of indoctrination and socialization. Should organizations therefore reject them altogether or is a compromise solution possible? In an organizational change context, the "subversive loyalist," is a change agent who has the best interests of the organization at heart, but does not feel constrained by existing norms and processes.[2] On the face of it, Perry Cox would seem to fit this model. He has no desire to destroy Sacred Heart. It is, after all, his entire life, perhaps to an unhealthy extent. So, can we translate this concept of "subversive loyalist" to the individual context? Provided a mentor always has the best interests of the learner at heart, does this mean the potential downsides of subversion will all be avoided? Tough love and even open derision by the mentor is OK, provided it is for the learner's own good?

Well, no, even from the limited and somewhat eccentric examples we have discussed here, it is clear that what separates constructive subversion from destructive subversion is actually an interlocking combination of factors, of which concern for the learner is just one.

SUMMARY

In the right context, and used responsibly, subverting the accepted order of things is a crucial part of the mentor's role in facilitating learning and change. This may be achieved through presenting alternative perspectives, challenging underlying assumptions, playing the sceptic, leading the learner out of their comfort zone and allowing them to feel the discomfort of uncertainty, or simply using humour to puncture and undermine perceptions of difficult people and situations, and point up absurdity and incongruity. In the cause of opening learners' minds to alternative interpretations of reality and ways of understanding the world, mentors might even "bend" some of the established codes of mentoring. But if we are to do this without damaging the confidence and self-esteem of our learners, or create havoc in the organizations that sponsor them, we must recognize the potential for harm, and pay heed to a number of key safeguards:

- The mentor must be *self-aware*, understand how they are perceived by others, and be able to recognize when their subversion stems from the desire to pursue some personal agenda or fixation.
- The mentor must be *honest about their intent*. They must have the best interests of the learner at heart.
- Having the organization's best interests at heart will not always be compatible with this, and may detract from the whole point of subverting the status quo. However, it would seem to make sense for a mentor to be clear with any sponsoring organization that *questioning the norm may be part of the process*, and ensure that, in Kessels' terms, they have an "open corporate curriculum."[4]
- The mentor must *match their approach to the learner*. What degree of subversion and challenge can they and the relationship stand? Not everyone is as puppy-like as J.D.
- The mentor should have good cause for questioning and undermining established convention, rather than sniping for the sake of it. In this sense, they must feel there is *good reason for tough challenges*.
- Mentors should be *strong positive role models* themselves in order for their questioning and challenge to be credible.
- Any subversion must be *additive not reductive*. In other words, it must generate further alternative options, rather than simply knock down

the existing ones. Questioning is helpful, but replacing one ortho-doxy with another is not.

- Finally, causing a learner to question a strongly-held assumption or belief creates a void. The subversive mentor must *step back* from filling this and *create the space* in which the learner can develop alternative ideas.

REFERENCES

[1]Sweeney, B. (2005). Mentoring: a matter of time and timing. In *Teacher mentoring and induction* (H. Portner, Ed.). London: Sage Publications.

[2]Clarke, M., & Meldrum, M. (1999). Creating change from below: Early lessons for agents of change. *The Leadership and Organization Development Journal, 20*(2), 70–82.

[3]Daloz, L. (1999). *Mentor,* San Francisco, CA: Jossey-Bass.

[4]Kessels, J. W. M. (2001). Learning in organizations: a corporate curriculum for the knowledge economy. *Futures, 33*(6), 497–506.

[5]Megginson, D., Clutterbuck, D., Garvey, R., Stokes, P., & Garrett-Harris, R. (2006). *Mentoring in action: A practical guide,* (2nd Ed.). London: Kogan Page.

Television, Films and Books

Lawrence, W. (Creator). *Scrubs* [Television series]. New York: ABC.

Neame, R. (Director), & Allen J. P. (Writer). (1969). *The Prime of Miss Jean Brodie* [Motion picture]. Los Angeles: Twentieth Century Fox. (Adapted by from her play of the novel by Muriel Spark [1961], published by Macmillan.)

Shore, D., & Attanasio, P. (Co-creators). (2004). *House* [Television series]. Beverley Hills, CA: Fox.

CHAPTER 7

ATTORNEYS, ALIENS AND FOOLS

Mentoring for Diversity and Speaking Truth to Power

KING LEAR

In Shakespeare's story, Lear is a king with three grown daughters. He decides to do what in today's parlance would be called going into early retirement; and to hand over the running of his kingdom to his daughters, allocating the share of power according to the degree to which they profess to love him. The youngest, Cordelia, although she genuinely loves her father, refuses to play this game, and is disowned and banished. Lear then divides his kingdom between the two remaining daughters, who have falsely professed their love and loyalty, and they proceed to strip him of his power and retinue, leaving him homeless and mad (in both senses of the word). By the time he recognizes that his decision-making has been based on deluded thinking, it is too late and the daughter who genuinely loved him is dead (along with just about everybody else). In corporate terms this is a classic mishandling of executive succession, not to mention a human resources nightmare of misdirected rewards and redundancies. The pointed jokes and well-disguised wisdom of his court jester are enough to bring the King eventually to his senses; but this comes too late to save the organization which was once his kingdom.

"You'd make a good fool," King Lear's jester tells him. Like all jesters worth their salt, he's making a play on words here. Jester and fool: in Shakespeare's time they both meant the same thing. What Lear's Fool is saying, in effect, is: "You're so foolish, it's you who ought to be called the Fool, not me." And he goes on, adding insult to injury:

> FOOL: If thou wert my fool, nuncle, I'd have thee beaten for being old before thy time.
> LEAR: How's that?
> FOOL: Thou shouldst not have been old till thou hadst been wise. (King Lear, 1:5)

In other words, "You shouldn't have got to the age you have without gaining a bit of common sense." A Fool's riddles – and we see this in several of Shakespeare's plays – are not just aimed at getting laughs; they are designed to make the hearer *think*, and, through thinking, arrive at some insight. These riddles serve the same purpose as the probing or challenging questions a mentor asks. They provoke reflection and present a fresh perspective on things. And what else is the Fool doing here, apart from risking some right royal rage or the loss of his head? One answer is that he is "speaking truth to power"; he is challenging the perspective of someone more powerful than himself so that a lesson may be learnt, or some degree of enlightenment achieved. This is an enterprise that takes some courage. The modern day equivalent might be an employee in the lower echelons of the organization conducting a mentoring dialogue with the chief executive and asking:

> So how do you think others see this decision you're taking?

Or:

> So what do you think might be the consequences for the way the company is perceived?

Or:

> It sounds as though you're saying that you'd hoped things would turn out differently?

These, of course, are ways a competent mentor would phrase the question. What lies behind this deceptively gentle enquiry may more closely resemble the question posed by Lear's Fool: "How did you get this old and stay this stupid?"

This chapter is about perspective and the role mentoring can play in challenging perspectives which are narrow, flawed, inaccurate or limited. We'll be looking particularly at relationships that we'll refer to as "*upward mentoring*," where the learner is in a position of power or is higher up the organizational hierarchy than the mentor. We'll be drawing what we hope is a clear distinction between mentoring which leads to genuine learning and change, and other types of support which, though they might present on the surface as mentoring, are really designed simply to disguise or compensate for a senior colleague's personal or professional failings. Perhaps most importantly, we'll be exploring the role that mentoring can play in challenging such learners' perceptions and pre-conceptions and helping them learn to value diversity and difference.

Perception, as any psychologist will tell you, is not all about what's actually out there. To a large extent it is we ourselves who impose order on the data our brains receive. For example, we only really perceive that which we give our attention to. There is just *too much data* out there for us to make sense of otherwise. And we make assumptions about what we see – assumptions based on our pre-existing beliefs and prejudices. This means that our perspective on ourselves and our world cannot in any sense be called "objective." Our perceptions come to each of us mediated through our own particular tangle of previous experiences, political and religious affiliations, likes and dislikes, and so on. A useful example here might be our understanding of what we mean by "an untidy house." From one individual's perspective, it might be the sight of toys and clothes all over the floor and three weeks' worth of dishes in the sink that tells them their house is untidy; for another, it might take only the sight of one ornament slightly out of place on the mantelpiece. Now obviously you wouldn't ever want to stay the weekend with either of these people; but the point here is that the way we perceive ourselves and others and everything around us reflects more than simply "what is." It reflects something about ourselves, too. It can become distorted or outdated or destructive – and yet we can still be there insisting that that's "the way things really are." This false certainty can pose a danger to ourselves and those around us, particularly if we are in a position of power. So let's begin by considering why the Fool gets away with – and is even encouraged in – challenging his King in the way he does.

WHY CHOOSE THE FOOL TO MENTOR THE KING?

This sounds like the start to a riddle, and in a way it is; but it is a riddle with several layers of answers. Translated into modern terms the question becomes: what might be gained by having a more junior colleague act as mentor for someone further up the organizational hierarchy? The most obvious answer to this is that the mentor will be able to bring a new perspective to bear. When you are looking down from the top, you will have a wider view, but objects on the ground will look small and may therefore appear insignificant. Closer to the ground you will see things very differently and in more detail. And if you happen to be one of those "insignificant" objects right down there on the tarmac, the view you have of the person looking down from the top will be very different from the view they have of themselves. Your perspective may not allow you to see them at all; or if it does they will certainly appear remote. Understanding that our own perspective is partial and subjective and needs to be challenged from time to time is essential to our learning and growth. Lear's Fool is attempting to jolt his king into getting a different perspective on things. This will involve Lear realizing that just because he's king, he isn't perfect; and that everything isn't always everybody else's fault. It will involve him in seeing the reality of the situation, which is that he himself is to blame. The Fool knows that a change of perspective can be enlightening – not only when you're in danger of alienating your nearest and erstwhile dearest – but also when you're trying to grasp the true significance of a situation, or to spot the contradictions lurking beneath an apparently compelling argument.

But what other benefits, apart from providing this fresh perspective, might such upward mentoring bring? In the case of Lear's Fool, his ability to challenge the king with impunity probably arises from the very fact that he *is* a Fool – albeit a wise one – and therefore poses no real threat to the King himself, only to his flawed way of seeing the world. Indeed, this mentor's apparent naiveté might be the very thing to catch his King at the most unguarded moment when his questions and riddles can really "get through" to him. Perhaps more crucially, though, this relationship works because both parties are clear about the "unconditional positive regard"[1] in which the Fool holds his King. There may be implicit criticism in his banter, but this doesn't mean that he is judging Lear. He accepts him for what he is. His affection and loyalty are not conditional on his master's behavior. As we have observed earlier, in Chapter Four, "unconditional positive regard" doesn't mean approval of everything the other person does. Here it means that the Fool, in his mentoring role, continues to genuinely care about his King *despite* Lear's faults. What is at work here is empathy, and this allows the mentor to understand at the deepest level how it feels to be Lear. The Fool mentors the King, therefore, from a spirit of acceptance and understanding, and not from a position of scorn or contempt for his superior's failures of judgement. And then, of course, there's the King's insanity; and, when the King is mad, the clear-sightedness of the Fool is bound to come in handy.

The answer to our riddle, then: "Why choose the Fool to mentor the King?" is threefold:

- Upward mentoring can encourage the adoption of *new perspectives*
- The non-threatening status of the mentor (and sometimes the appearance of naiveté) can be helpful in *penetrating defences*
- The mentor can *build trust* by exhibiting unconditional positive regard and genuine empathy

It is for such reasons that upward mentoring has already been used to good effect in well-known multi-national companies and government departments. It is not difficult to see how bosses at the top of an organization might become remote from what is going on "at the coal-face." One of the benefits of mentoring from below is that it provides what have been called "friends in low places" – a window on aspects of the organization that the more senior leader may seldom see, or even insights into technological changes that may have passed them by.[2]

BLIND MEN AND FOOLS

Lear's tragedy is that he is *blind* to the truth. His perception of himself and those around him is fatally flawed. In a chapter which focuses on challenging limited, outdated or mistaken perspectives, his story makes a useful metaphor. Indeed, blindness, figurative and otherwise, is a motif which runs throughout the play. Lear's old friend Gloucester, who has been metaphorically blind to the virtue of his good son, favouring instead his corrupt bastard, is literally blinded, in a very uncomfortable scene, by one of Lear's deeply unpleasant daughters. This inability to see clearly, both real and symbolic, leaves Lear and Gloucester profoundly disabled when it comes to finding a way out of the chaos they have helped create. Lear's "blindness" takes the form of self deception and a failure to think through to the consequences of his actions. His perspective on the world is awry.

One indicator of this is that the way he views himself is *completely at odds* with the way he is viewed by others. He sees himself as a powerful and benevolent king, respected by two daughters, wronged by the third; whereas in fact he's really a deluded and despised old despot who destroys the only child who loves him. There is also a dissonance between his professed aims and the tragic outcomes of his actions. He wants to enjoy retirement by letting his daughters and sons-in-law take the strain; and mistakenly assumes he will still be able to enjoy the status, regard, loyalty and sway that have hitherto been his by right. Instead, the outcome is that he is entirely abandoned and dispossessed. He thinks to measure his children's loyalty and worth by requiring that they give speeches itemizing the details of their love for him. The outcome is that spin wins, and the genuinely loyal child remains silent on principle. We can add another discrepancy to this list, too: that between the values Lear professes to hold and the behaviors he exhibits. He claims to value honesty and loyalty, but misjudges and disowns his only loyal daughter. Lear's perceptions are distorted, and, not least, his perception of himself. He is what we'd call today a terrible judge of character. And the Fool is the mentor whose thankless task is to help this retired chief exec towards a more realistic and accurate view both of the world and of himself.

Lear's Fool is not alone. There is a long literary tradition of utilizing the viewpoint of the outsider, the joker, the innocent abroad to jolt us, the readers, into a sudden and illuminating recognition of the world as it really is. From Candide, Gulliver and Alice, to Iain Banks's *Whit*[3], this device of seeing things with new eyes can be used to throw light on aspects of politics, economics, religion or social relations which we have come to take for granted through habitual exposure. When we are allowed an outsider's-eye-view we are more likely to see contradictions or absurdities which familiarity and custom have rendered invisible. An enlightening example of this – from real life, not from fiction – is cited by Umberto Eco, author of *The Name of the Rose* whom we've met already in Chapter Two. He relates a true incident about a group of anthropologists visiting France from another continent and being astonished to find that people there *took dogs out for a walk*[4]. Being encouraged to look with new eyes at something which we have hitherto taken for granted as simply "the way things are" can be an important step in *recognizing that there may be other assumptions or perceptions driving our behavior or decision-making which have remained too long unexamined.*

MENTORING FOR DIVERSITY

Seeing things from a new perspective – from *another's* perspective – is often called for when mentoring for diversity. Current practice across commercial, public and government sectors indicates that such mentoring systems are increasingly being put in place in order to raise awareness of issues relating to multiculturalism, gender, youth culture, and so on. These are areas where the challenges to stereotyping or blinkered thinking have to come from the bottom up in order to bring about learning and change at senior levels. This is about helping the learner to gain insight into the feelings or circumstances of individuals or groups who are different to themselves in some way. This difference may be one of class, race, ethnicity, gender, rank, physical attractiveness, age, ability, income, health, disability, culture, sexual orientation, political persuasion, or some other area of difference, equally relevant and important. Like those anthropologists whose cultural background meant that they had never before thought of dogs as needing any help or structure with something so obviously natural to them as walking about, so might someone from a dog-walking culture feel shocked to find dog on a restaurant menu. These are not questions of right or wrong, but of cultural difference. Adjusting to such differences and accommodating them within our world view is a necessary part of the process of individual learning and growth. A chief executive who expressed the view that anyone who ate dog should be shot would not only be severely limiting their company's international relations but would also, by publicly espousing the view that "different" is "wrong," be failing to give an appropriate lead in terms of company values. Such a manager would be in urgent need of mentoring; and hopefully some brave Fool would be there to do it.

SHIFTING PERSPECTIVES: *MEN IN BLACK*

All this talk of an alien's eye view and getting a whole new perspective on dogs brings us neatly to the 1997 film, *Men in Black*, directed by Barry Sonnenfeld, and starring Tommy Lee Jones and Will Smith as Agents K and J. Experienced agent, K, takes on newly appointed agent J as his sidekick in the mission to manage the presence of aliens on Earth in such a way that the human population remains unaware of the extraterrestrials living everywhere among them. Some of these aliens are harmless; others – the "bugs," including a giant sentient cockroach who takes human form – are here with evil intent. It is K, the senior agent, who opens Agent J's eyes to this situation.

So far, then, this is a classic mentoring relationship, with the more experienced operative acting as mentor to the rookie. K is helping J to see the world in whole new way. It is one in which there is a constant danger from death rays; in which aliens live unsuspected among us and include various celebrities in their number, such as Sylvester Stallone; in which a standard galactic week is one hour long; in which a dog can be an alien diplomat and a galaxy can be small enough to fit inside the jewel on a cat's collar. Perhaps most astonishing of all it is, J finds, a world in which sensationalist tabloids are the most accurate source of intelligence.

People in general are simply unaware of what is going on, largely because the Men in Black are able to induce amnesia with their "neuralyzer": an instrument the size of a pocket torch which also enables them, through the power of suggestion, to substitute an alternative explanation in people's minds for the circumstances they find themselves in (such as covered in blue alien goo). Their "blindness," as far as alien presence goes, is not self-induced as King Lear's is. But just as Shakespeare does in *King Lear*, this film explores questions of perspective – and far less grimly, it must be said. In the famous opening sequence we are shown a dragonfly's view of its lengthy flight to earth from space and into a city and along a highway.... only to have our point of view cut suddenly to inside a speeding car with the dragonfly splatted on the windscreen. This is one way of telling us that the way things look depend on where you're standing and whether you're aware of the bigger picture.

This is a lesson which Agent J learns quickly. And, even as he is adjusting his own world view, he begins to take on a mentoring role himself, challenging his senior partner, Agent K, to reflect on certain aspects of his practice. Very early on he tells K that his "people skills" need working on. It is clear to us as audience that he is quite right. K's interpersonal manner is brusque and insensitive at best. And so J proceeds to draw his attention to the need for respect when dealing with the public, and to the possibility of creating more convincing alternative "truths" for those on the receiving end of the neuralyzer. Each agent, therefore, encourages the other to shift their perspective, but in different ways. There is an emotional deficit in K, despite his superior knowledge and experience. His junior partner helps him to recognize this and address it. It may even be that J's mentoring is responsible for K's eventual decision, once the immediate alien threat is averted, to prioritize love over work and to hang up his black suit and go back to his wife.

There are clear parallels here to Lear and his Fool. Both these relationships involve upward mentoring; in both, the senior of the two is suffering because of their failure to see or acknowledge flaws in the way they interact with others; and in both stories the mentor, the junior partner, enacts the role of clown to get under the learner's defences. Above all, however, both are tales about perspective. They show how our view of the world (and our place in it) may well be only partial, or be flawed in some other way; and they illustrate the importance of having our perspective questioned and challenged from time to time, in order that we can learn and grow.

FROM MAD KING TO MAD COW: MENTORING AND DIFFERENCE IN *BOSTON LEGAL*

By the end of *Men in Black*, we realize that Agent K has been grooming Agent J to succeed him. The mutual mentoring which has taken place within their partnership has clearly worked well both ways. We can see a relationship in some ways similar to this operating between Denny Crane and Alan Shore in the American TV series, *Boston Legal*. Denny Crane, played by William (Captain Kirk) Shatner, is a senior partner in the law firm Crane, Poole and Schmidt, and has been, in his time, a master of courtroom strategy and a great celebrity in the world of legal practice. Now, alas, his useful days are numbered. He has been diagnosed as suffering from early stages of Alzheimer's disease (which he refers to as "mad cow"), and his behavior has become unpredictable and sometimes bizarre. He is still able to coast by, however, on the strength of his magnificent reputation, despite the decline in his mental acuity and his tendency to disregard the law. In fact, we could say that he is a largely benign and quite endearing version of Lear. He is a man used to power and the deference of others; used to getting what he wants, and used to being listened to; but whose grasp of reality has become so flawed that he can no longer see himself or the consequence of his actions clearly.

Alan Shore, played by the excellent James Spader, is certainly adept at acting the fool when he chooses. As a maverick lawyer working for the same firm, he befriends, counsels and mentors Denny, enabling the elderly lawyer to continue to practice despite his bouts of memory loss, his frequent inability to grasp the details of cases and his often inappropriate behavior. As the series progresses it becomes clear that these two genuinely care for each other. Their relationship goes beyond that simply of colleagues with a mutual professional interest, and enters another category altogether: that of a close and loving friendship in which each demonstrates his "regard" for the other. It is a relationship which benefits them both and enables them both to learn. Alan simplifies and explains complicated cases for Denny, who in turn is able to share with Alan a lifetime of useful contacts and a masterly grasp of courtroom tricks.

And yet these two characters are *different* in so many ways. Alan votes Democrat while Denny votes Republican; Alan embraces values of egalitarianism and social justice while Denny's values are reactionary, capitalist and right-wing; Alan is sharp, bright, witty, and socially competent while Denny is losing his edge and – to an increasing extent – his mind. These differences go side by side with significant similarities which may account in part for the firmness of their friendship. Both are blunt and plain-speaking with clients and colleagues; both are subversive and rebellious, each in their different way. Alan refuses to conform to ways of seeing which lead to complacency or injustice. Denny simply refuses to conform; and one suspects that many of his eccentricities may be nothing to do with his dementia, but that his tendency to harass any woman he encounters, and to shoot anyone who annoys him, have always been integral to who he is.

Their differences, including their disparity in status, do not prevent them from developing a deep mutual respect for one another. This mutual respect puts Alan in the position of being able to challenge his senior partner's eccentric perspective and "blind spots" without appearing to be challenging or judging the man himself. And yet, despite his uncritical acceptance of Alan, Denny shows himself to be deeply intolerant of difference in most other contexts, notably those of politics and religion. His blinkered perceptions certainly do need challenging at times, particularly when he is articulating extreme and reactionary views. So here again we have a character who has much to gain from some upward mentoring.

As well as mutual trust and respect, there is a further factor which contributes to Alan's success in his mentor role. As we've seen, he and Denny appear, on the surface of things, to share very few values, assumptions or beliefs. If we accept Gerard Egan's view[5] that we use our values as the criteria on which we base our decision-making, and that the decisions we make are what consciously drive our behavior, we can understand both how Denny Crane's errors of moral judgement arise, and also how Alan Shore, with his secure and passionate adherence to a more ethical set of values, is ideally equipped to help him. As we have noted elsewhere[6], effective mentoring necessitates the mentor having clear insight into their own values and beliefs. It follows from this that the mentor needs to reflect upon these occasionally, for the simple reason that beliefs and values can shift and change with time. For Alan Shore, his role as a lawyer, and his regular performances in court to argue for principles of social justice and ethical practice, mean that he is regularly required to identify and consider his own values and moral stance. This conscious awareness and regular review of his own values lends greater strength to Alan as an effective mentor.

Undoubtedly some people can live perfectly comfortably with a limited perception of what's going on around them, as long as there are no drastic consequences for themselves or others. As with most other things, there are greater and lesser degrees of flawed vision. Egan[5] lists five "degrees of unawareness." These are the types of unawareness which lead to blind spots, and must be recognized, acknowledged and overcome if a new, clear-sighted perspective is to be achieved. Denny Crane, sad to say, works his way through all five of them as the series unfolds. They are:

- Simple unawareness;
- Failure to think things through;
- Self-deception;
- Choosing to stay in the dark; and
- Knowing but not caring, and failing to see the consequences.

There is surely a tragic irony here in that – although we suspect that Denny has always had a blinkered view of things – each one of these progressive failures of awareness could equally be attributed to the worsening symptoms of his dementia. We may blame Denny's "mad cow" or Lear's madness (for the old king exhibits exactly the same range of unawareness); but these types of limited vision by no means apply only to the elderly and afflicted. Only think of the senior manager, head teacher or public sector executive who is:

- Simply unaware of what is going on in some corner of the organization; or
- Even worse, makes a decision without recognizing the probable knock-on effects; or
- Worse still, tells themselves that everything's bound to be alright (even though it clearly isn't); or
- Perhaps worst of all, prefers not to be told if things are going badly wrong; or, knowing, underestimates the implications and the consequences.

These are circumstances in which effective mentoring, upward or otherwise, can challenge perceptions which limit effectiveness and growth. Denny may prefer to stay in the dark or not to think things through, or even to deceive himself, when it comes to a question of his illness. Like many of us at some time or another, he may prefer not to see the world as it really is because such a vision would be too painful to bear. This is the thinking that informs the use of the Men in Black's amnesia-inducing neuralyzer: that the human population will only be able to continue with their day-to-day lives if they remain unaware of the ubiquitous alien presence. And Lear, of course, having persisted so long in his wilful blindness, is driven mad when the delusion falls away and he is forced to see clearly what he has done. Distorted perception, in other words, is often bound up with *fear of the consequences of facing reality*.

MENTORING UPWARDS – THE STORY SO FAR

We have looked so far at some of the purposes of upward mentoring and seen how these are often linked to bringing about a change of perspective in the learner – as in mentoring for diversity – and an encouragement to embrace and value difference rather than reject or fear it. We've also considered some of the factors which enable upward mentoring to work effectively, and seen that these depend on the skills and attributes of the mentor and on the non-judgemental, non-threatening relationship which they are able to establish with the learner. Perhaps it is no coincidence that the learners in the stories we've chosen for this chapter are all either mad or totally lacking in social skills, or both. It would be unfortunate, however, to say the least, if this were to create the impression that everyone at the top is awkward or insane; or indeed if it were taken to suggest that it is only in extreme cases of dementia or social ineptitude that such mentoring is called for. This is, of course, not the case. These afflictions provide vivid metaphors for the inability to see things as they really are; while a failure of empathy and an inability to relate appropriately to others may indicate some difficulty with the concept of inclusion and the valuing of difference. This makes them particularly useful examples in a chapter such as this one.

But before we all rush off to help the boss, it's important to remember that not all help directed "upwards" qualifies as effective "mentoring." This is particularly so when the support is made necessary by the failures or deficiencies of the senior partner. In cases like this, a more accurate way to describe what is going on is "compensation." This is where the junior partner of the two is compensating – or possibly even covering – for the inefficiencies, inadequacies or plain old incompetence of their senior. We can see this distinction clearly if we look for a moment at that famous fictional partnership: the Rt. Honorable Bertie Wooster and his trusty manservant, Jeeves.

WHAT THE BUTLER SAW: MENTORING OR RESCUING?

The all-knowing and ultra-efficient Jeeves and his over-privileged, dim but pleasant employer, Wooster are comic characters invented by the English novelist P. G. Wodehouse and have been most recently portrayed on the small screen by Stephen Fry and Hugh ("House") Laurie. A typical Jeeves and Wooster plot involves the capable manservant solving some problem or muddle that Bertie Wooster has become involved with. Such muddles often involve a risk of bringing down the wrath of one of Bertie's formidable and aristocratic Aunts.

In each of these episodes it is certainly the case that Jeeves demonstrates many of the qualities and skills of an effective mentor, notably:

- Sensitivity;
- Professionalism;
- Tact;
- The ability to demonstrate unconditional positive regard for Bertie
- Responding to Bertie's agenda rather than imposing his own; and
- Never pointing out directly to Bertie that he is wrong (except in matters literary).

Here, Bertie Wooster represents a deficient "boss" or superior whose perspective and understanding are limited. In this sense he can be equated with King Lear, or Denny Crane (or even Agent K in his bungling of human relationships). But, as the episodic and familiar format of the stories indicates, *Bertie never learns*. A typical comment while Jeeves is carefully explaining something to him in the short story, *Indian Summer of an Uncle* (1930) tells us that Bertie has no serious intention of learning or changing or broadening his perspective in any way. Of Jeeves's explanation he says:

I saw that this was going to take some time. I tuned out.

Having handed the situation over to Jeeves, then, he feels absolutely no need to try and understand it for himself. And this is partly Jeeves's fault. He repeatedly and reliably solves Bertie's problems for him. He advises him what to do, rather than encouraging or enabling him to come up with solutions himself. In Jeeves's and Wooster's working relationship there is no encouragement for Bertie to reflect; and yet it is reflection which is necessary if he is to arrive at any insight. Therefore the possibility here of insight leading to action is remote. Bertie and his behavior remain unchanged. And his perspective on the world, although repeatedly challenged by Jeeves's successful interventions, never shows any sign of changing, either. And why would it have to, if Jeeves is always there to do his thinking for him?

But wait! Isn't this what we saw Alan Shore doing with Denny Crane? Well, we don't think so. Alan and Denny's working relationship rests on mutual respect. Alan never loses sight of Denny's previous achievements as a lawyer. Very rarely does Alan step in to *rescue* his friend; rather he encourages and *supports*. Denny Crane is still capable of insight; he is able on occasion to step outside himself and recognize the extent to which his powers have deteriorated. He is still, with Alan's help, capable of learning and positive change. In other words, he is still able to link his rare insights to action.

This serves to remind us that effective mentoring requires a collaborative endeavour. It isn't something "done to" the mentored partner; it's something the partners work through together. For all that Jeeves demonstrates his possession of some mentoring skills, Bertie Wooster, most of the time, simply takes instruction from him. It's not so much that Bertie has blind spots; it's that he's simply not very bright. But this isn't the only reason why he never learns. He doesn't grow, develop, or show any sign of learning because he is never made to think things out for himself. All he does learn is that it's okay to turn to Jeeves every time there's a problem, and that Jeeves will sort it out. Despite this astonishingly persistent help and support which Bertie receives from his manservant – support which continues (in literary terms, at least) for over fifty years, from 1919 to the 1970s – there isn't any real mentoring going on here at all. Moreover, it would probably be fair to say that in this partnership it's the boss who's the fool – though a likeable one. Jeeves, then, makes a useful model only insofar as he demonstrates sensitivity and professionalism. Beyond this, his approach – that of intervention, direction, and "saving the day" – is one to be avoided by mentors. Unless, that is, they have some vested interest in keeping an incompetent, vacuous nincompoop in post.

SUMMARY

So, can a mentor provide effective support to someone who is quite different from themselves, whether in terms of rank, moral disposition or world view? Is it going to be possible for them to challenge the perspective of a senior colleague or someone in a position of power? The answer we have arrived at in this chapter is: yes and yes, it would seem they can. But, in addition to the usual requirements, like demonstrating empathy and "unconditional positive regard," such upward mentoring will be more effective when it conforms broadly to the following criteria:

- Differences in status/power can be overcome or ignored.
- A safe space can be created in which both parties can openly challenge.
- The project is one of mutual growth rather than of rescue.
- The mentor is clear about their own values and beliefs.
- The learner's "blind spots" are identified and challenged.
- The focus is not on covering up or compensating for inadequacies but on learning.

We've seen that it is often possible to recognize when a learner's perspective is dangerously limited or flawed by the fact that they may, like King Lear and Denny Crane:

- Have a view of themselves which is glaringly at odds with the way they are viewed by others.
- Be the cause of outcomes which are contradictory to their expressed aims.
- Be unable to assimilate positively into their world view notions of difference and diversity.

The mentor's task of speaking truth to power is not an easy one. It rests crucially on encouraging the powerful to reflect on their view of the world, and, in doing so, bring about what transformation may be necessary. For most of us (hopefully), what limits or distorts our perspective is not Lear's delusions of power or the Men in Black's neuralyzer, but ourselves. The assumptions and pre-conceptions which influence our decision-making may need more regular re-examination; and for this we may need to overcome a fear common to most of us, of unflinchingly facing up to things as they really are.

REFERENCES

[1]Rogers, C. (1983). *Freedom to learn for the 1980s.* London: Merrill.
[2]Clutterbuck, D. (2004). *Everyone needs a mentor* (4th Ed.). London: CIPD.
[3]Banks, I. (1995). *Whit,* London: Abacus.
[4]Eco, U. (1993). *Misreadings.* London: Picador.
[5]Egan, G. (2002). *The skilled helper* (7th Ed.). Pacific Grove, CA: Brooks/Cole.
[6]Wallace, S., & Gravells, J. (2007). *Mentoring,* Exeter: Learning Matters.

Television, Films and Books

Kelley, D. E. (Creator). (2004–2008) *Boston Legal.* [Television series]. New York: ABC.
Shakespeare, W. (c1603). *King Lear.*
Sonnenfeld, B. (Director). (1997). *Men in Black.* [Motion picture]. Universal City, CA: Amblin Entertainment.(Based on the comic strip by Lowell Cunningham, published by Aircel Comics.)
Wodehouse, P. G. (1930). *The Indian Summer of an Uncle.*

CHAPTER 8

"GET BUSY LIVING OR GET BUSY DYING"

Purpose, Autonomy and the Power of Positive Thinking

THE SHAWSHANK REDEMPTION

When we first see Andy Dufresne, he is sitting in his car, removing a pistol from the glove compartment. In the next scene he is being handed down two life sentences for the murder of his wife and her golf pro lover. The year is 1947.

The central relationship in *The Shawshank Redemption*, a film by Frank Darabont, adapted from a Stephen King short story, is essentially one of mutual learning and support. It takes place in Shawshank, the Maine penitentiary, to which the court has consigned Andy, a vice-president of a large Portland bank, and it comprises his growing friendship with "Red," an old lag, who has already been inside for twenty years. Apart from his encyclopaedic knowledge of prison life, Red's main attribute is getting his hands on illicit goods the "cons" want smuggled into the jail.

Something of an epic tale, (movie-speak for very long), *The Shawshank Redemption* has grown in popularity since its release, to become, at the time

111

of writing, number one in IMDb's ranking of the greatest films of all time. It's not hard to see why. Quite apart from the on-screen chemistry of the two leads, Tim Robbins and Morgan Freeman, and the fact that we all love a good prison break yarn (from *The Great Escape* to, well, *Prison Break*), the enduring appeal of this tale is its message about the redeeming power of hope. OK, it's not a subtle message. In fact it clubs us over the head as often as the sadistic Captain Hadley. But, unlike Captain Hadley, its power to make us feel good is undeniable.

At first, "Red" does not really rate Andy Dufresne. As the new intake of inmates arrive and cynical cons bet on who will cry first, "Red" has his eye on the lanky, elitist milksop, Andy. But he is proved wrong that first night, and for the next twenty-odd years, as Andy not only survives the brutal and de-humanizing world of Shawshank, but succeeds in maintaining his self-respect and integrity, and keeping alive his dream of escape and freedom. At first, "Red" (full name Ellis Floyd Redding) acts as Andy's guide to the unwritten rules of prison life and the characters, in both types of uniform, who prowl its galleries and exercise yards. He helps Andy adjust to the routines, and later supports him through periods of physical and mental suffering at the hands of both "Bogs," a vicious sodomist, and his gang of "Sisters," and the prison authorities, who commit Andy to solitary confinement repeatedly, for his various small, but significant acts of rebellion. There is also a strong implication that "Red" is at least partially instrumental in Andy's "de-frosting," his transformation from cold fish, a hard man who, by his own admission, did not display enough emotion towards his wife, into a much warmer human being, who values friendship and takes trouble to return small kindnesses and make sacrifices for others. That this humanization should take place in the de-humanizing environment of Shawshank penitentiary is a neatly ironic touch, and goes to the heart of this "triumph over adversity" parable.

But in Andy and Red's relationship the learning is decidedly mutual, and most significant is the impact Andy has on "Red." For all the pragmatic guidance "Red" affords Andy, his outlook, conditioned by years of repeated rejection at parole hearings, is one of resignation, low expectations and scraping by. He has allowed himself to get too accustomed to life inside, and what Andy offers him is an alternative perspective. Andy keeps his hope of escape and his dream of a beachside hotel and charter fishing boat alive for twenty long years. For most of this time Red sees such hope as dangerous and undermining, but eventually he comes to respect and appreciate it as a force for survival and ultimate redemption.

If you began reading this chapter wondering what on earth a prison movie might have to do with mentoring, well, let's just re-cap on those themes:

- What is truly important in life – Real happiness and how to achieve it.
- The triumph of hope and optimism over fear and despair.
- Persistence in the face of disaster.
- Being true to yourself.
- Avoiding dependency and maintaining one's autonomy.

Every one of these is a topic which can help us to think about our own mentoring practice.

HARBINGER OF HOPE OR PROPHET OF DOOM?

For a mentor, these opposing points of view are hugely significant, as they speak directly to the twin demands we all face of encouragement, hope and support on the one hand, and questioning, challenging and facing up to reality on the other.

> MENTOR: Gary's enthusiasm was infectious. When I first started mentoring him, I was taken aback by his sheer chutzpah. Broken home, multiple run-ins with the police, a dearth of conventional qualifications....These are not ideal conditions under which to nurture ambitions of business success. But Gary remained undaunted. There were times when I felt his expectations of how quickly he could establish an independent record label were unrealistic, and I saw it as my responsibility to challenge him quite hard. Then, looking back, I wondered whether I had been guilty of squashing the very force that was keeping him going against all the odds....

> MENTOR: Becky has a lot going for her. She is bright, creative and likeable. But she gives up easily. For her, if she's tried something once and not got the result she wanted, then she's "failed," and there's no point continuing with that course of action. The idea that anything worth having is worth battling for seems to escape her. I want to buoy her up and find ways to bolster her resolve, but I find myself more often getting dragged down into her slough of despond. Helping her remain positive in the face of setbacks, without resorting to pathetic platitudes is a challenge.....

ACCENTUATE THE POSITIVE: THE CASE FOR THE DEFENCE

Let's start by looking more closely at the gospel according to Andy Dufresne. Despite two life sentences for a crime he did not commit, multiple beatings, two years of regular gang-rape, spells of solitary, and the murder of his young protégé and the only man who could prove his innocence, he does not succumb to despair. In fact he spends twenty years tunnelling through his cell wall and into the prison sewer with a small rock hammer (courtesy of Red's procurement skills), finally crawling to freedom through 500 yards of pre-digested prison food. His response to eventually receiving some books for the prison library, after six years of weekly letters to the authorities, is to start all over, writing *two* letters a week instead of one, and he braves the wrath of Warden Norton by playing Mozart over the public-address system because it reminds him that there is something inside him that the brutal-izing prison regime cannot touch. Truly, this is positive thinking on a mythi-cal scale. Rather like those images of Rita Hayworth, Marilyn Monroe and Raquel Welch that cover his twenty-odd years of tunnelling, Andy is himself a poster-boy for positive psychology, albeit a couple of decades before his time.

Ryff et al.[1], expanding on the work of Marie Jahoda[2], cite six conditions that correlate with psychological well-being:

- Autonomy
- Environmental mastery
- Personal growth
- Positive relations with others
- Purpose in life
- Self-acceptance.

Well, we have referred already to the *personal growth* Andy undergoes in prison, with Red's help, and this is partly about establishing *positive relations with others*, particularly young Tommy Williams whom he tutors through his high school diploma. He undoubtedly has a *purpose in life*, which is to escape from Shawshank, trick the Warden out of his ill-gotten gains, buy his hotel and charter his fishing boat. As for *self-acceptance*, he comes to terms with his own behavior, acknowledging that, as a cold and unfeeling hus-band, he indirectly had a role in his wife's death, despite not actually being the one to pull the trigger.

This leaves *autonomy* and *environmental mastery*, two tricky states to achieve you might think, whilst banged up in the gothic purgatory that is Shaw-shank. And yet, as Andy demonstrates, psychological resilience can be all about small victories. So he exercises his *autonomy* and *environmental mastery* in a number of ways:

- He finds a way to use his expertise – helping prison staff with finan-cial advice.
- He fights for resources for the prison library – putting his intelli-gence and business skills to work for the greater good.
- He defies the authorities by playing Mozart over the public-address system.

- He never sacrifices his integrity, and stands up to Warden Norton at the price of yet another spell of solitary.

So, the first thing we can observe about Andy is that he demonstrates all of the behaviors that positive psychology might correlate with well-being, in spite of circumstances being somewhat against him. The second thing to note is his *persistence*. He simply does not give up; whether it's protesting his innocence, not giving in to Bogs and "the Sisters" or digging through several feet of concrete. As Red points out, when they finally discover the hole in the wall behind the poster of Raquel Welch, Andy's hobby – geology – is a perfect metaphor for this approach to life and its misfortunes. It's the "study of pressure over time." Andy does not just sustain his hope and self-belief, he also perseveres in methodically implementing his plan, in spite of barriers and setbacks. One can read all sorts of messages into this, both religious and secular. The pursuit of real happiness is not about hedonistic seeking after material gain and pleasure. Andy presumably had this in his previous life as a wealthy banking executive, and look where it got him: sitting in a car contemplating murder while his wife carries on with her golf pro. Andy's reward, in the guise of his new life in paradise, comes after years of purgatory in Shawshank, during which he uses his skills for the greater good and remains true to his real self. Take away the religious connotations and this could be a story about how any happiness worth achieving requires coming to terms with one's true self, behaving authentically and consistently with this, appreciating one's responsibilities towards others and persisting in sticking to one's purpose, even in the face of calamity. The ancient philosophers referred to this vision of happiness as "eudamonia" (as opposed to hedonism, or the simple seeking after pleasure).[3]

It should be pointed out, before we all get too dewy-eyed, that Andy also ends up with $370,000 worth of the Warden's money, which presumably sweetens the preceding twenty years of enforced, aesthetic self-denial somewhat. But if this is not about mentors helping clients eschew their lives of material comfort and go live in a cave contemplating the wickedness of earthly pleasures, then can we distill some more practical lessons from the gospel according to Andy Dufresne?

- **Establishing purpose** – Many writers on mentoring have emphasized the importance of clear goals, whilst others have more recently questioned how they are used. What the Shawshank story suggests is that, whatever the learner's particular situation, helping them to clarify their purpose is partly about helping them to identify what true happiness and satisfaction (as opposed to simple pleasure) means for them. This requires us to talk about values and beliefs, the things that are of abiding importance to us, not just the biographical data of what passes for normal social intercourse. Such conversations can be awkward, but without them we cannot help to construct goals which are congruent with our learner's true self, and the fulfilment of which will therefore bring real happiness.

- **Removing fear** – One of the common barriers between a learner and fulfilment of their purpose – one source of what Myles Downey calls interference – is fear: fear of the unknown, fear of failure, fear of disappointment[4]. We all find ourselves sometimes, like Red, para-lysed, imprisoned, unable or unwilling to take action in pursuit of our dreams because we fear what having our hopes dashed might do to us. Part of the mentor's response to this might be reinforcing the learner's confidence and self-esteem. But we can also learn to re-frame our mistakes and setbacks as part of learning and therefore part of progress. Then setbacks can be not just endured, but even valued, and what Red calls "shitty little pipe dreams" can eventually prevail.

- **Maintaining autonomy** – We have highlighted the perils of creating dependency in a mentoring relationship in Chapter Three. The reverse side of this coin is what the mentor does to actively promote autonomy. This begins, as above, with helping the learner build their self-awareness, understand who they are, what they value and what they believe in. From there, it extends to ensuring that the mentor-ing focuses on what is within the learner's control, and that their actions are consistent with their self-image and their principles. There are many events in our lives that we are not able to control. Andy Dufresne has no control over the decision to incarcerate him in Shawshank, nor over most of the indignities and cruelties that are visited upon him during his 20-year sojourn there. Purpose and goals and planning are all well and good, but randomness and accident are also a feature of life. So, like Andy, we exercise our free will not only in the way we actively make things happen in line with our goals, but also in how we respond to the unexpected over which we have no control. Whatever life throws at us, we can still retain our auton-omy over how we react to it. In his book, *The Luck Factor*,[5] Richard Wiseman cites "turning your bad luck into good" as one of his four principles, (after "maximising opportunities," "following your intui-tion" and "expecting the best").

Finally, maintaining autonomy involves knowing when allowing a learner to struggle for answers, however counter-intuitive, is absolutely the respon-sible course of action. Compare Andy's well-preserved sense of indepen-dence with the institutionalization of Brooks Hatlens, the elderly prison librarian he finally takes over from. Brooks is paroled after 40-odd years of incarceration, only to find that he is incapable of adjusting to life outside

Shawshank. Finally, he hangs himself. As Red sees it, inmates begin by hating the prison walls, then get used to them, and finally come to depend on them; a fate he almost falls prey to himself when finally released. In Andy we see someone made *more* determined by imprisonment to fulfil his dreams and more capable of doing so, whereas in Brooks we see someone crippled by dependency on an environment that he has allowed to dictate his every move and thought. As mentors, we are always striving to help bring about Andy Dufresnes, and avoid creating Brooks Hatlens. In the final analysis, our goal is to provide processes and structures by which our learners can eventually mentor themselves.

- **Investing in relationships** – As mentors, we can help learners understand their impact on others, help them to find ways of maintaining reciprocal, emotionally intelligent relationships, where they give and request help freely, and help them to appreciate the benefit of mutually supportive networks in persisting with scary challenges in the face of difficulty. Not only this, but we can also help them to learn from these challenges, successful or otherwise. These are all aspects of the mentor's role which might appear peripheral, but are actually central to learner well-being.

- **Persisting against the odds** – This is yet another element of "positive mentoring" which we might recognize in our own practice. Emphasizing successes over failures, re-framing experiences in a more positive light, occasionally acting as conscience or cattle prod to remind learners of actions not yet addressed, asking for examples of successful endeavours: all approaches and interventions we may deploy as mentors to inspire our learners to pick themselves up, dust themselves down and start all over again.

But, we don't just have to take the word of a fictional character for all this. A wealth of compelling research suggests strong links between optimism, a more positive outlook, and good health, perseverance in problem-solving, career success, and leadership.

Martin Seligman, one of positive psychology's best-known thinkers, has written of ways in which those of us not blessed with a naturally sunny outlook can consciously adjust what he calls our "explanatory style" in order to respond to negative events in a more positive, and by implication, more constructive way.[6] By questioning our beliefs about adversity and its consequences, by forcing ourselves to dispute evidence and generate alternative explanations, we can start to re-frame the impact of such negative events, so that they appear temporary, impersonal and limited to specific chance circumstances, as opposed to permanent, personal to us, and all-pervading. If people can have this conversation with themselves, then how much more effective might it be if conducted with a skilled mentor? So there is strong evidence that practical and effective methods exist by which a mentor can help a learner imprisoned in an Ellis Redding place take a more Andy Dufresne perspective.

STEADY ON NOW: THE CASE FOR THE PROSECUTION

At this point, you may be thinking,

> All well and good, but, as a mentor, I can't just spend my whole life offering people hope and extinguishing their fears. Surely I have a responsibility also to help people to think through the potential consequences of their actions, and make informed decisions about the future, based on a realistic assessment of risks and pitfalls? If I don't occasionally help them to identify the negatives, they might take risks they can ill afford.

So, is there room in the mentor's psyche for a bit of Ellis Redding as well as Andy Dufresne; a bit of good, old-fashioned pessimism as well as Andy's unshakeable resolve? If you suggested to most learners that you might provide them with a pessimistic mentor, I imagine they would be less than enthusiastic. But what if we replace the word "pessimism" with the word "realism"?

Interestingly, research suggests that pessimists actually tend to have a more accurate grasp of reality than do optimists.[6] (If this piece of information depresses the bejesus out of you, you're probably an optimist. If it fills you with a certain sense of pride, then it's likely you're a pessimist). One might reasonably argue that an accurate perception of reality is as important an element of psychological good health as any of these other factors we have been discussing up to now. Certainly, it is hard to deny that mentors can prove very helpful in challenging assumptions and prompting learners to think through the consequences of decisions, weighing up pros and cons and recognizing potential risks before embarking on a course of action. If we accept that coaching can be a role mentors adopt when required, then we cannot ignore the fact that one of the most widely-used coaching models (GROW) begins with a comparison between goals and reality.[7] Surely, applied judiciously and in the appropriate circumstances, this sceptical questioning has got to be a legitimate part of our role?

Moreover, helping people overcome their natural pessimism might seem an entirely positive idea, but how does playing around with someone's underlying view of life square with helping them be true to who they are? With something as central to our decision-making process as our natural optimism or pessimism, there must be dangers inherent in messing with a learner's explanatory style? Seligman has his own thoughts on balancing "learned optimism" with appropriate doses of reality. He identifies a phenomenon known as "complex optimism," which consists of recognising when the future can be changed by more positive thinking, and adjusting one's explanatory style accordingly, but avoiding undue optimism where this is not the case. The problem with this argument is that, condemned to two life sentences in Shawshank, you might be forgiven for assuming that positive thinking was unlikely to change the future. This is essentially the conclusion that Red has reached.

MAYBE MESS WITH MISTER IN-BETWEEN?

In mentoring there are two parties to the conversation, so this must be partly about the dynamic. What are the implications, both good and bad, of the respective levels of optimism/pessimism in the mentor and her learner? We have tried to represent this in Figure 8.1. As we consider the possible combinations of mentor and learner, it becomes apparent that, whatever the mix, there are potential dangers to be aware of (in bold italics), but also benefits that could accrue (in standard text). Clearly, optimism and pessimism are on opposite ends of a continuum, rather than absolute states, and so our diagram depicts extremes. Arguably, the relationships with the most potential for harm, whether from Tigger-like euphoria, or Eeyore-like despair, are those where mentor and learner share the same extreme positive or negative viewpoint.

	MENTOR	
	Pessimist	*Optimist*
MENTEE *Pessimist*	***Plummeting self esteem. Fail to question negative assumptions. Avoid risks / opportunities*** Play optimist–Challenge self–limiting beliefs. Generate options for action	***Encourage more risk than tolerable. Skip evidence & analysis*** Challenge defeatist self-talk & dispute negative assumptions
Optimist	***Discourage, miss opportunities, stop risk-taking*** Ask about options & consequences, reality check	***No reality check. Fail to consider range of outcomes*** Play pessimist–force analysis of pros & cons

FIGURE 8.1. Optimism and Pessimism in Mentoring Relationships.

It is hard to conclude anything other than that what is required of mentors here is a degree of balance. More than this, even, is that we need to be able to adopt alternative perspectives, and to recognize when these are appropriate. Crude though it may be, frameworks like that above may give us some guidance as to how and when to accentuate the positive or suggest a reality check.

STAR WARS – FEEL THE FORCE

There are six films altogether in the *Star Wars* franchise, but here we are choosing to concentrate on the first two, now called IV and V, rather than the subsequent, slightly confusing array of sequels and prequels. *Star Wars Episode IV – A New Hope* is the first, and most fondly remembered of George Lucas's great oeuvre, and introduced us to the evil Galactic Empire, the Rebel Alliance and the mysterious properties of the Force. Its sequel, *Star Wars Episode V*, retains many of the characters we came to love in the ground-breaking first film, plus a few new ones, and has a somewhat darker tone. After a lukewarm initial reception, it has come to be seen by many as the best of the series. What particularly interests us here is that both films are partly about the power of positive thinking and both revolve around important learning relationships.

In *Star Wars Episode IV* we are introduced to Luke Skywalker, a restless youth, living on the planet Tatooine with his aunt and uncle, in the middle of what appears to be an enormous desert. His uncle wants Luke to help with the "harvest" (What of? – sand?), but Luke has dreams of escaping his humdrum existence. When his uncle buys two droids captured by Jawas, the sackcloth-clad midgets who live in a big skip on wheels, Luke discovers the mayday message left by captured rebel leader Princess Leia for Obi Wan Kenobi, a retired Jedi Knight. Luke goes off to deliver the message to Obi Wan, and is drawn into the galactic power struggle, learning to be a Jedi with the help of his patrician mentor, Obi Wan, the sublime Alec Guinness.

MENTOR ONE: OBI WAN

As mentors go, Obi Wan is reasonably non-directive (except when he's telling Luke to use the Force, which he does quite a lot). In spite of the urgent need to go to Alderaan and rescue Leia, not to mention his Jedi mind control power to make people do what he wants them to anyway, Obi Wan actually leaves Luke to do what *he* thinks is right. Throughout the film, and despite being dead for a large portion of it, the venerable Jedi fulfils several other mentoring roles, acting as role model to Luke, in negotiating with

Han Solo for example, coaching Luke in the use of the light sabre, and helping him understand the "bigger picture" of inter-galactic politics and power struggles. But most importantly of all, Obi Wan introduces Luke to "the Force," the importance of faith and of trusting his intuition.

For, like *The Shawshank Redemption*, this is a story about overcoming huge obstacles and seemingly impossible odds in order to achieve your dream, but here it is portrayed as a futuristic version of the mythical quest. A young man sets out on a dangerous journey to rescue a fair princess, and along the way is transformed into a hero.

Although, thanks to Luke, the Death Star is successfully destroyed at the end of Episode IV, the threat of the Empire has not been eliminated, and Episode V sees the Rebel Alliance holed up on the ice planet of Hoth, being attacked once again by Darth Vader's storm troopers. All our old friends are there. The android C-3PO still minces about wittering inconsequentially. Han Solo still grins roguishly whilst tinkering about on the Millennium Falcon with an oily rag, like it's a 30 year-old Morris Minor, and even Obi Wan is still visiting ghost-like from the afterlife, dispensing words of wisdom. But now Luke is sent off to Dagobah and introduced to a new mentor in the form of the small, reptilian sourpuss, Yoda.

MENTOR TWO: YODA IT IS

We will avoid getting into a debate about whether Yoda is a mentor or a coach, although his relationship with Luke does seem to be a peculiar mix of lessons in moral philosophy and faintly sadistic physical jerks (running through the jungle with Yoda on his back, balancing on one hand with Yoda on his foot, etc.). We will also choose to ignore the fact that the first thing Luke's new mentor does is lie to him, by not revealing his identity, and that his "unconditional positive regard," is hardly exemplary, as he chides Luke somewhat dyspeptically at every opportunity. But, since his reward for training Jedi knights for the past 800 years is to live all alone in a deserted swamp, it is perhaps not surprising that Yoda is a bit of a crotchety old fart. And, amongst all the ludicrous physical training and mystical mumbo-jumbo, Yoda does help Luke overcome his self-limiting beliefs and apply the power of positive thinking.

PERSISTENCE, SELF-BELIEF AND
THE PRESUMPTION OF SUCCESS

He berates Luke for giving up too easily, for not believing he can achieve the tasks he is set. He explains to him that success is partly a state of mind, and that attaining the degree of self-belief needed will involve "unlearning what he has learned," abandoning some of his negative assumptions about what is possible. There are echoes of *The Matrix* here, as Yoda exhorts Luke to stop trying and "do." In other words, he must believe that he is capable of performing the exercises, rather than just doing the best he *thinks* he can. When Luke expresses his disbelief at Yoda's telekinetic raising of the jetfighter from the swamp, Yoda tells him that this is the very reason for his failure.

Belief in a positive outcome is not the only lesson either. Like Andy Dufresne, Yoda subscribes to the view that overcoming overwhelming odds is also about persistence and strength of resolve. Luke is warned that choosing the "quick and easy path" may leave him vulnerable to becoming an "agent of evil." It is because Luke has not entirely mastered his control of "the Force" that Yoda and the spirit of Obi Wan try to prevent him flying to the rescue of Han Solo and Princess Leia, who have been betrayed by Lando Calrissian and captured on the gas mining colony of Cloud City. But the young Jedi wilful and impetuous is, and a two-foot green man and a hologram not much to stop him can they do. So Luke goes off to fight Darth Vader, discover he is his father, and get his hand chopped off, before being rescued by Leia and Han in the Morris Falcon.

THE "FORCE" AND "FLOW"

In both films, Luke finally saves the day by overcoming his doubt and fear of failure and using "the Force." At the end of Episode IV he manages to deliver a missile into the only small chink in the Death Star's defences; the equivalent of dropping a cigarette butt down a lavatory from a fighter travelling at three hundred miles an hour. By the closing credits of Episode V he may have gained an unwanted father and lost a rather more useful hand, but he has still survived a duel with the Sith Lord and escaped his wicked trap without succumbing to the "dark side." Leaving aside the mysticism, telepathy and telekinesis, "the Force" has a lot in common with the phenomenon known in positive psychology as "flow." Indeed, Obi Wan actually tells Luke that a Jedi can feel the Force flowing through him.

"Flow" is a term coined by Mihaly Csikszentmihalyi in his book of the same name about what provokes enjoyment.[8] His research indicates that we experience "flow" when we are so totally engaged in an activity that we lose all sense of time and the worries of everyday life, and our thoughts and actions feel effortless. We might be engaging in a sport, giving a talk, playing music, or dropping a bomb into a Death Star. What the experiences will have in common is a heightened sense of fulfilment and self-actualization. According to Csikszentmihalyi, achieving "flow" requires a number of conditions to be present:

- It must be in pursuit of a task we have a chance of completing.
- We must be able to *concentrate* on what we're doing.

- The task should involve *clear goals* and *immediate feedback.*
- We act with deep but effortless involvement shutting out the doubts and worries of everyday life.
- We're able to exercise a degree of *control* over our actions.
- Our concern for self disappears, but our sense of self is reinforced.
- Our sense of time is altered.

Achieving "flow" enables us to have "mastery over consciousness," a concept one suspects both Yoda and Obi Wan would recognize. The idea behind "flow" is that an approach to success and happiness that necessitates the control of external circumstances to meet our particular goals is always demanding and frequently utterly impossible. As our inmates at Shawshank discover, we are frequently not in control of external events. What can prove far more productive and satisfying is changing how we experience those external circumstances to make them fit our goals better. Thus Andy Dufresne finds "flow" in his music, his petitioning for the prison library, and his tunnelling, while Luke finds "the Force" in his jetfighter flying and a little light sabre rattling. In Csikszentmihalyi's view, our chances of experiencing "flow" are much improved if we are able to respond to adversity by transforming negative external conditions into a subjectively controllable experience. We do this by:

- Focusing on details and finding opportunities for action.
- Setting ourselves achievable goals, and getting feedback on progress.
- Using courage, resilience, and perseverance to turn negative events into positive opportunities.

This theory takes Maslow's idea[9] – that self-actualization requires the satisfaction of basic needs first – and suggests that, in fact, if it is subjective experience that is seen as real life, rather than so-called objective reality, then we can achieve optimal experience in even the direst of physical circumstances: an idea that I imagine Andy Dufresne would wholly support.

SO, WHAT CAN WE LEARN...?

What then are the common threads that we can tease out from these stories and the lessons they hold about positive psychology? What are the implications for how we practice as mentors?

At the heart of every mentoring dialogue is achieving a mutual understanding of the relationship's purpose, based on a robust discussion about what constitutes real happiness for the learner and what is truly important in their life. This will involve helping our learner to develop their

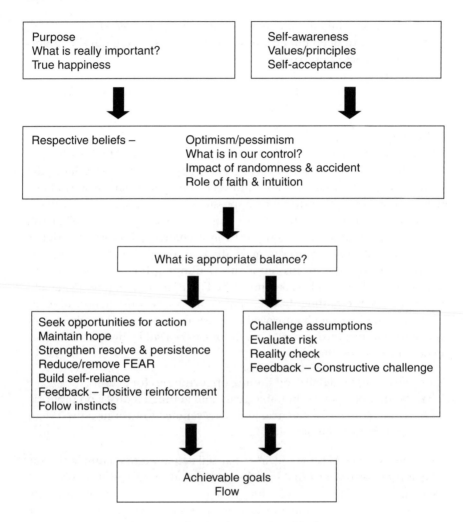

FIGURE 8.2. Achieving Self-actualization and "Flow."

self-awareness and construct an honest picture of their values, their virtues and their allowable weaknesses with which they can feel comfortable.

Following this, there needs to be some discussion by which both parties arrive at a better appreciation of each other's respective levels of optimism/ pessimism, their beliefs about what is in our control and the impact of randomness and accident, along with the role of faith and intuition in their decision-making. Is it the mentor's role partly to help their learner to trust their "inner voice," and, if so, can we automatically assume that everyone's "inner voice" is equally accurate and reliable? Without this, we are in danger of applying a "one-size-fits-all" approach to our learners, assuming either that everyone needs positive thinking or everyone needs a stern reality check, depending most likely on our own life view exclusively.

Armed with a clearer view of the dynamic at play within the learning partnership, however, we stand a much better chance of appropriately balancing the undoubted benefits of positive psychology with what may be entirely apposite doses of risk analysis and assessment. On the one hand, we could be helping our learner seek opportunities for taking action where they can exert control, maintain hope in the face of adversity, bolster their resolve and persistence, remove fear of failure, build self-reliance and follow their instincts. On the other, we might be challenging their assumptions, helping them evaluate risks, or sharing a reality check. In both cases we might offer feedback, carefully assessing the need for balance between positive reinforcement and constructive challenge.

As a result of following a process like that shown in Figure 8.2, mentoring partners should encounter more success in identifying and working towards goals that are both achievable and challenging, as well as congruent with the learner's sense of self. Furthermore, these goals will fit better with a learner's true concept of happiness and entail activities and events over which the learner has genuine control. All of this should increase the likelihood of persevering against adversity and achieving optimal experience or "flow" and thereby self-actualization.

REFERENCES

[1]Ryff, C. D., & Singer, B. H. (1998). Emotion, social relationships and health, *Psychological Enquiry, 9,* 1–28.

[2]Jahoda, M. (1958). *Current concepts of positive mental health,* New York: Basic.

[3]Peterson, C. (2006). *A primer in positive psychology,* New York: Oxford University Press.

[4]Downey, M. (2003). *Effective Coaching,* New York: Texere.

[5]Wiseman, R. (2003). *The Luck Factor,* London: Random House.

[6]Seligman, M. (1990). *Learned Optimism,* New York: Random House.

[7]Whitmore, J. (1992). *Coaching for Performance,* London: Nicholas Brealey.

[8]Csikszentmihalyi, M. (1992). *Flow,* Harper & Row, USA.

[9]Maslow, A. (1970). *Motivation and Personality* (2nd Ed.). New York: Harper and Row.

Television, Films and Books

Darabont, F. (Writer/Director). (1994). *The Shawshank Redemption* [Motion picture]. United States: Castle Rock Entertainment. (Loosely based on a novella by King, S. (1982). *Rita Hayworth and Shawshank Redemption.* New York: Viking Press.)

Lucas, G. (Writer/Director). (1977). *Star Wars Episode IV: A New Hope* [Motion picture]. United States: Lucasfilm.

Kershner, I (Director), & Lucas, G. (Writer). (1980). *Star Wars Episode V: The Empire Strikes Back*. United States: Lucasfilm.

CHAPTER 9

SUMMARY

We now reach the end of this foray into the world of fictional learning partnerships, and the observant reader will have noted that no mention has been made of the film that inspired our title, *Dial M for Murder*, Alfred Hitchcock's classic 1954 thriller, starring Ray Milland and Grace Kelly. Whilst making it into the American Film Institute's Top Ten mystery films, and providing a catchy title for a book on mentoring in popular culture, it sadly lacks anything resembling a mentoring relationship.

However, if we have learned one thing about stories, in this context, it is that they often reward the effort of coming at them from a different angle. Hitchcock's thriller famously revolves around the central character's idea that one can design the perfect murder. Tony Wendice, an ex-professional tennis player (played by Ray Milland), has spent over a year planning to murder his wife, meticulously eliminating every possible slip that might lead to his detection and capture. He stages a fake blackmail plot against his wife, over a letter written to her American lover, Mark Halliday; forces an old university acquaintance to carry out the deed, having spent months withdrawing tiny sums in used notes with which to pay his accomplice; and sets up an alibi for himself by attending a stag party in a nearby hotel. For a while, his fiendish plot seems watertight, albeit Byzantine to the point of stupefaction.

But, as his wife's lover, a thriller writer himself, points out: planning the perfect murder is one thing; carrying it out successfully relies on people behaving in exactly the way you have planned them to. Sadly for Tony Wendice, hardly anyone does what they are supposed to, including him. His wife refuses to stick to her routine of listening to the radio in her bedroom, his watch stops, delaying his vital phone call, Swann, the hitman, replaces the key to the flat under the stair carpet, the slim and elegant Mrs. Wendice turns out to have the strength of an all-in wrestler and inconveniently stabs Swann with some scissors, and Tony, despite some clever recoveries, is left trying inconspicuously to shift £1000 in used notes. (These days he could just pop into the post office and pay last month's energy bill.)

In the course of these eight chapters, we have looked at a few reasonably good mentors and a host of frankly scary ones. But if one were avidly to apply all the learning from this and every other book on mentoring, could one become the perfect mentor and design the perfect mentoring session? Well, *Dial M for Murder* has it pretty much spot on. Any attempt to ensure perfection in an activity which relies on the way people behave when responding to each other's words and actions is doomed to failure, whether that activity be mentoring or murder. This is also why meticulously planning a mentoring conversation can be a dangerously unproductive endeavour. Because, in real life, unlike on screen, people never stick to their lines, and the exchange that went so well in our heads may take a sudden nosedive when the other party responds in an unexpected way. If there is a recurring theme from the preceding pages, it is that control, certainty and one-size-fits-all solutions are at best unhelpful, and sometimes downright dangerous concepts in any learning dialogue.

In using *stories* to encourage growth and self-discovery, it is as a *non-directive* narrative that they can prove most helpful. They allow us the freedom to adapt elements of them to our own circumstances, and consider multiple interpretations of our own experiences, based on different assumptions and values from those that come naturally to us. Think of how Ninny Threadgoode's stories of jumping freight trains and braving bees help Evelyn to escape the tyranny of others' expectations and forge a life of her own.

The process of *learning* is often about opening our minds to *multiple realities*, and this can be best served by maintaining a state of not knowing, encouraging learners to accept doubt and ambiguity as part of continuous learning and enquiry. Helping people learn how to develop *choices* and *options* for action is one of the most rewarding outcomes of mentoring. Think of William of Baskerville shining the light of enquiry into the labyrinthine library of the Benedictine abbey, with its one, jealously-guarded, "truth," its forbidden books and its intolerance of competing ideas.

The worst excesses of *manipulation and abuse of power* in learning relationships begin with an urge to *control*. This undermines trust, imposes unwanted agendas, and sabotages the learner's sense of agency, leading to dependency on the part of the learner and dissembling by the mentor. Think of the vampire Lestat and his doll-like woman-child, Claudia, trapped in a resentful and ultimately destructive partnership.

Mentors will have their own individual *values and moral boundaries*, which will inform their choices about supporting and enabling particular learners. Mentors may legitimately want to challenge assumptions and actions. They may also wish to avoid becoming *complicit* in behavior which is inimical to their own values. But it is not their role to convert, or to replace the learner's own *conscience*. Think of Jennifer Melfi, becoming complicit in the murderous and brutal activities of Tony Soprano by unwittingly enabling him to rationalise and justify his behavior and lifestyle in the context of his own distorted moral code.

Mentors must also be clear about the way they view the possibilities and processes of *personal change*. It is not their place to hold out false hopes of "self actualization" nor to mislead the learner into assuming there are quick fixes and short cuts to self fulfilment. Think of Captain Picard supporting the android, Data, helping him to recognize that although the *possibilities for change may be limited* and the *process of change is demanding*, the journey towards personal fulfilment is nevertheless worthwhile.

A mentor may choose to be deliberately *subversive* in order to question taken-for-granted assumptions and *challenge the status quo* (or enable others to do so). But the purpose of this is always to generate further alternative options rather than to replace one orthodoxy with another. The *subversive mentor* creates a void which they must then help their learner to fill with their *own* alternative ideas. Think of the redoubtable Jean Brodie undermining the stuffy school curriculum in favour of more universal concepts of beauty, romantic love, and dedication to a cause, only then to fill her pupils' receptive young minds with her own idealistic admiration for goose-stepping "fascisti."

It may be part of a mentor's role to "*speak truth to power*" by challenging the *perspective* of someone at the top. This *upward mentoring* cannot be done effectively unless the mentor is prepared to regularly examine their own assumptions and pre-conceptions. Neither will it be effective if the mentor simply attempts to cover or compensate for the flaws of the learner. Think of Jeeves, whose constant interventions mean that his employer never succeeds in learning anything.

When we draw upon the ideas of *positive psychology* in our mentoring it is important for mentor and learner to understand each other's beliefs about the impact of *randomness and accident,* and what is genuinely within their sphere of control. The way each party's beliefs and thought processes incline them to a more *optimistic or pessimistic* reaction to events will affect the dynamic between mentor and learner. This, in turn, will determine the most helpful way for the mentor to respond to the learner's needs, balancing positive thinking with an appropriate analysis of risk. Think of Andy Dufresne and "Red" Redding, men with very different outlooks on how to respond to life's adversities, helping each other find the courage and persistence to prevail against all the odds and escape from Shawshank to their tropical paradise.

So, as mentors, what we can do is spend time reflecting on our practice, continuing to learn how we relate to others, and trying to understand the behavioral, ethical and moral considerations behind the helping role we try to fulfil. This helps us to widen the repertoire of responses available to us when faced with each individual's take on the transitions, dilemmas and development needs facing them. Improving our responsiveness, rather than our planning, is probably the best preparation we can undertake. It will not have escaped your notice that few, if any, of the mentoring dilemmas reflected on in the preceding chapters lend themselves to any form of consensus solution. In some cases we have offered an opinion or suggested ways of reflecting on your own practice, and in others we have left the final conclusion to you. Because in most cases the appropriate response will depend, to some extent, on the personality, values and conscience of the individual mentor, and on how they relate to their learner. Perhaps the best that we can do as mentors is, like William of Baskerville, to reflect on the issues and dilemmas raised by our experiences, continually learning without necessarily expecting to pin down definitive right answers. At least then we are able to be transparent with our learners, even if it is only about our own uncertainties and questions. If we subscribe to a truly developmental model of mentoring, then leaving our learners not with a set of correct answers, but with the capability to continue independent questioning, reflection and learning is ultimately the measure of our success. We sincerely hope that our own small collection of stories has enabled you to gain some insight into how you manage some of these dilemmas and ambiguities, and thereby deepened your understanding of your own mentoring practice.

FILM

Hitchcock, A. (Director), & Knott, F. (Writer). (1954). *Dial M for Murder,* [Motion picture]. Burbank, CA: Warner Bros.

INDEX